# About this book

Military conscription and democratic norms do not make easy bedfellows. The right of the state to give orders to its citizens can clash with the citizen's right and duty to exercise moral and political judgement. In the case of Israel, hundreds of soldiers called up to take part in controversial campaigns or assignments (like the 1982 invasion of Lebanon, or policing duties in the Palestinian territories) have refused orders. In the current Palestinian intifada, over a thousand such refusals have been registered, many of the 'refuseniks' serving prison sentences rather than taking part in what they regard as an unjust occupation in defence of illegal Jewish settlements, an occupation that threatens the peaceful existence of their fellow Israelis.

In this inspirational book, Peretz Kidron, himself a refusenik who made this tough choice, gives us the stories, experiences, viewpoints, even poetry, of these courageous conscripts who believe in their country, but not in its actions beyond its borders. Here is a great spectrum of Israelis – officers and ordinary footsoldiers, men and women, from every ethnic background and class. Here is the story of Yesh Gvul ('there is a limit'...), the organization that has long served refuseniks as a voice and campaigning vehicle, as well as the newer refusal groups.

We read about the cautious, even embarrassed, response of the Israeli authorities. And we see the wider implications of the philosophy of selective refusal – which is by no means the same thing as pacifism – for conscientious citizens in every country where conscription still exists. Here is a real model for the peace movement in Israel and worldwide.

# ● About the editor

Peretz Kidron was born in Vienna in 1933. Months after the Nazi occupation of Austria, his family fled to Britain. On graduation from high school, he emigrated to Israel where he lived for 20 years in Zikim, a border kibbutz near the Gaza Strip, where he grew oranges, taught in a school, and engaged in voluntary work. A freelance journalist, broadcaster and writer, he has translated many books, including the memoirs of Yitzhak Rabin and Ezer Weizman, and a biography of David Ben Gurion. In 1976 he co-authored with the Palestinian activist, Raymonda Tawil, her memoirs, *My Home, My Prison*.

In the late 1960s, he became active in the radical left and the peace movement. He is a founding member of the Israeli Council for Israeli–Palestinian Peace and serves on the steering committee of the human rights watchdog B'tselem. Having refused to perform military duty in the occupied Palestinian territories, he now handles international contacts for Yesh Gvul ('There is a limit [to what an army can ask of its conscripts]'). Founded at the time of the invasion of Lebanon in 1982, the group has become the voice and campaigning vehicle for the so-called refuseniks – Israeli army reservists who report for duty when summoned but refuse morally objectionable assignments (notably serving in the West Bank and Gaza).

# Refusenik!
## Israel's Soldiers of Conscience

Compiled and edited by
**Peretz Kidron**

Foreword by
**Susan Sontag**

**Zed Books**
LONDON & NEW YORK

*Refusenik! Israel's Soldiers of Conscience* was first published by
Zed Books Ltd, 7 Cynthia Street, London N1 9JF, UK and
Room 400, 175 Fifth Avenue, New York, NY 10010, USA in 2004.

www.zedbooks.co.uk

Cover designed by Lee Robinson/Ad Lib Design, London N19
Typeset in 10/12.6 pt Bembo by Long House, Cumbria, UK
Printed and bound by Gutenberg Press, Malta

Distributed in the USA exclusively by Palgrave Macmillan, a division of
St Martin's Press, LLC,175 Fifth Avenue, New York, NY 10010

A catalogue record for this book
is available from the British Library

US Cataloging-in-Publication Data
is available from the Library of Congress

ISBN   Hb   1 84277 450 6
       Pb   1 84277 451 4

# Contents

● **Foreword** · Susan Sontag     xi

● **Introduction:**
**Israel's Refusenik Movement** · Peretz Kidron     1

● **The Early Refuseniks**     11

*Balance* • Yitzhak Laor     11

*Saying 'no' loudly and clearly* • Ishai Menuchin     13

*An artist at Ansar* • Zvi Goldstein     15

*Discovering the Palestinians* • Mike Levine     16

*In solidarity with the almond trees* • Peretz Kidron     17

● **The First *Intifada***     23

*I'm no martyr* • Hanoch Livneh     23

*Whatever the price* • Rami Hasson     24

*The problem is in Jewish society* • Menahem Hefetz     26

*Refusal to collaborate* • Dudu Palma     27

*I am an Arab Jew* • Meir Amor     28

*Father and son: refuseniks* • Carlos and Amit Levinhoff     30

*Spiral of evil* • Stephen Langfur     31

*The limit is human life* • David Ovadia     32

*The privilege of saying 'No!'* • Adi Ofir     35

*Silences that cry out* • Doron Vilner     39

*Benighted fanaticism* • Nitzan Levy     40

*A typical 'NO' poem* • Nathan Zach     41

*A policy that demeans my country* • Shaul Schwartz     41

*The refusenik answers the writer* • Mario Weinstein in
    correspondence with Yizhar Smilansky     42

*On the festival of freedom I waive my freedom*
        *Or: What shall I tell my daughter?* • Dubi Hayun    45
*No to 'Always at Command'* • Danny Zamir    46
*'You don't have to do anything wicked'* • Daniel Padnes    50
*Decent people don't shoot children* • Itamar Pitovsky    52
*I owe my children at least one refusal* • Dan Sagir    53

● **The Philosophy of Selective Refusal** • Peretz Kidron    55

● **The Story of Yuval and Imad**    61

● **The Second *Intifada***    71
*Letter to the editor of Koteret Rashit from Dov Barak*    72
**STATEMENTS BY JAILED CONSCRIPTS**    75
*Those who enlist and those who don't* • Uri Yaakovi    75
*Militarism and racism have reached a fascist level* • Haggai Matar    76
*I am a prisoner, yet free* • David Haham-Herson    77
*A violent and racist society* • Itamar Shahar    79
**STATEMENTS BY JAILED RESERVISTS**    82
*Vile injustice* • David Enoch    82
*The red line* • Michael Sfard    83
*Collaboration makes me a criminal* • Ro'i Kozlovsky    86
*A cause which is not mine* • Alex Lyakas    87
*An enormous 'black flag'* • Avner Kochavi    89
*A letter to the commander of Battalion 719* • Ehud Shem Tov    89
*I killed three innocent civilians* • Idan Kaspari    92
*The shattered dream* • Omry Yeshurun    95
*The IDF teaches that it's okay to molest an Arab* • Ishai Sgi    100
*Black Flag* • Itai Haviv    101
*Three exercises in refusal* • Ishai Rosen-Zvi    103
*Is Marwan Barghouti your uncle?* • Itai Ryb    107
*Why am I mad at the IDF?* • Ron Gerlitz    109

● **Closing Statements**    115
*My reply to the General* • Yigal Bronner    115
*Israel today is a prison* • Matin Kaminar    117

● **List of Addresses**    119

# ● Boxes

| | |
|---|---|
| Don't Go to Their War | xix |
| Occupation Means Murder | xxi |
| 'The Black Flag of Illegality' | 2 |
| I Cannot Take Part in Your Crimes | 9 |
| Bring the Soldiers Home! | 15 |
| General, Your Tank is a Powerful Vehicle | 21 |
| Joint Declaration of Yesh Gvul and Beit Sahour | 29 |
| Yom Kippur Plea for Forgiveness | 34 |
| Born on the Fourth of July | 49 |
| The Alternative Independence Day Ceremony | 69 |
| Letter from the *Shministim* to prime minister Ariel Sharon | 74 |
| Declaration of Refusal | 82 |
| We Won't Take Part! | 84 |
| 'Courage to Refuse' Declaration | 88 |
| The Occupation: a Curse on Both Peoples | 97 |
| Seder of a Thousand Refuseniks | 99 |
| Soldier, It's in Your Hands! | 102 |
| Yesh Gvul *Survival Kit for Refuseniks* | 106 |
| The Gaza Bombing was a War Crime! | 113 |

Dedicated to
Tal, Danya, Amit and Yonatan

# ● Foreword*

## Susan Sontag

Allow me to invoke not one but two, only two, who were heroes – among millions of heroes. Who were victims – among tens of millions of victims.

The first: Oscar Arnulfo Romero, Archbishop of San Salvador, murdered in his vestments while saying mass in the cathedral on March 24, 1980 – twenty-three years ago – because he had become 'a vocal advocate of a just peace, and had openly opposed the forces of violence and oppression' (I am quoting from the description of the Oscar Romero Award, being given today to Ishai Menuchin).

The second: Rachel Corrie, a twenty-three-year-old college student from Olympia, Washington, murdered in the bright neon-orange vest with Day-Glo striping that 'human shields' wear to make themselves quite visible, and possibly safer, while trying to stop one of the almost daily house demolitions by Israeli forces in Rafah, a town in the southern Gaza Strip (where Gaza abuts the Egyptian border), on March 17, 2003. Standing in front of a Palestinian physician's house that had been targeted for demolition, Corrie, one of eight young American and British human-shield volunteers in Rafah, had been waving and shouting at the driver of an oncoming armored D-9 bulldozer through her megaphone, then dropped to her knees in the path of the super-sized bulldozer ... which did not slow down.

Two emblematic figures of sacrifice, killed by the forces of violence and oppression to which they were offering non-violent, principled, dangerous opposition.

---

* Keynote address delivered in Houston, Texas, on 30 March 2003, on the occasion of the Rothko Chapel Oscar Romero Award to Ishai Menuchin, Chairperson of Yesh Gvul, the Israeli organisation formed to support refuseniks.

xi

## We are all conscripts

Let's start with risk. The risk of being punished. The risk of being isolated. The risk of being injured or killed. The risk of being scorned.

We are all conscripts in one sense or another. For all of us, it is hard to break ranks; to incur the disapproval, the censure, the violence of an offended majority with a different idea of loyalty. We shelter under banner-words like justice, peace, reconciliation that enrol us in new, if much smaller and relatively powerless, communities of the like-minded. That mobilize us for the demonstration, the protest, the public performance of acts of civil disobedience — not for the parade ground and the battlefield.

To fall out of step with one's tribe; to step beyond one's tribe into a world that is larger mentally but smaller numerically — if alienation or dissidence is not your habitual or gratifying posture, this is a complex, difficult process.

It is hard to defy the wisdom of the tribe: the wisdom that values the lives of members of the tribe above all others. It will always be unpopular — it will always be deemed unpatriotic — to say that the lives of the members of the other tribe are as valuable as one's own.

It is easier to give one's allegiance to those we know, to those we see, to those with whom we are embedded, to those with whom we share — as we may — a community of fear.

Let's not underestimate the force of what we oppose. Let's not underestimate the retaliation that may be visited on those who dare to dissent from the brutalities and repressions thought justified by the fears of the majority.

We are flesh. We can be punctured by a bayonet, torn apart by a suicide bomber. We can be crushed by a bulldozer, gunned down in a cathedral.

Fear binds people together. And fear disperses them. Courage inspires communities: the courage of an example — for courage is as contagious as fear. But courage, certain kinds of courage, can also isolate the brave.

The perennial destiny of principles: while everyone professes to have them, they are likely to be sacrificed when they become inconveniencing. The cry of the anti-principled: 'I'm doing the best I can'. The best given the circumstances, of course.

## No, I will not serve

Let's say, the principle is: it's wrong to oppress and humiliate a whole people. To deprive them systematically of lodging and proper nutrition; to destroy their habitations, means of livelihood, access to education and medical care, and ability to consort with one another. That these practices are wrong, whatever the provocation. And there is provocation. That, too, should not be denied. ·

At the centre of our moral life and our moral imagination are the great models of resistance: the great stories of those who have said 'No'. No, I will not serve.

What models, what stories? A Mormon may resist the outlawing of polygamy. An anti-abortion militant may resist the law that has made abortion legal. They, too, will invoke the claims of religion (or faith) and morality – against the edicts of civil society. Appeal to the existence of a higher law that authorizes us to defy the laws of the state can be used to justify criminal transgression as well as the noblest struggle for justice.

Courage has no moral value in itself, for courage is not, in itself, a moral virtue. Vicious scoundrels, murderers, terrorists may be brave. To describe courage as a virtue, we need an adjective: we speak of 'moral courage', because there is such a thing as amoral courage, too. And resistance has no value in itself. It is the *content* of the resistance that determines its merit, its moral necessity.

Let's say: resistance to a criminal war. Let's say: resistance to the occupation and annexation of another people's land.

Again: there is nothing inherently superior about resistance. All our claims for the righteousness of resistance rest on the rightness of the claim that the resisters are acting in the name of justice. And the justice of the cause does not depend on, and is not enhanced by, the virtue of those who make the assertion. It depends first and last on the truth of a description of a state of affairs which is, truly, unjust and unnecessary.

Here is what I believe to be a truthful description of a state of affairs that has taken me many years of uncertainty, ignorance, and anguish, to acknowledge.

A wounded and fearful country, Israel is going through the greatest crisis of its turbulent history, brought about by the policy of steadily increasing and reinforcing settlements on the territories won after its victory in the Arab war on Israel in 1967. The decision of successive Israeli governments to retain control over the West Bank and Gaza, thereby denying their Palestinian neighbors a state of their own, is a catastrophe – moral, human, and political – for both peoples.

The Palestinians need a sovereign state. Israel needs a sovereign Palestinian state. Those of us abroad who wish for Israel to survive cannot, should not, wish it to survive no matter what, no matter how. We owe a particular debt of gratitude to courageous Israeli Jewish witnesses, journalists, architects,

poets, novelists, professors – among others – who have described and docu-
mented and protested and militated against the sufferings of the Palestinians
living under the increasingly cruel terms of Israeli military subjugation and
settler annexation.

Our greatest admiration must go to the brave Israeli soldiers, represented
here by Ishai Menuchin, who refuse to serve beyond the 1967 borders.
These soldiers know that all settlements are bound to be evacuated in the
end.

These soldiers, who are Jews, take seriously the principle put forward at
the Nuremberg trials in 1946: namely, that a soldier is not obliged to obey
unjust orders, orders which contravene the laws of war – indeed, one has an
obligation to disobey them.

### An obligation to disobey

The Israeli soldiers who are resisting service in the Occupied Territories are
not refusing a particular order. They are refusing to enter the space where
illegitimate orders are bound to be given – that is, where it is more than
probable that they will be ordered to perform actions that continue the
oppression and humiliation of Palestinian civilians. Houses are demolished,
groves are uprooted, the stalls of a village market are bulldozed, a cultural
centre is looted; and now, nearly every day, civilians of all ages are fired on
and killed. There can be no disputing the mounting cruelty of the Israeli
occupation of the 22 percent of the former territory of British Palestine on
which a Palestinian state will be erected. These soldiers believe, as I do, that
there should be an unconditional withdrawal from the Occupied
Territories. They have declared collectively that they will not continue to
fight beyond the 1967 borders 'in order to dominate, expel, starve and
humiliate an entire people'.

What these soldiers have done – there are now some two thousand of
them, more than two hundred and fifty of whom have gone to prison – does
not contribute to tell us how the Israelis and Palestinians can make peace,
beyond the irrevocable demand that the settlements be disbanded. The
actions of this heroic minority cannot contribute to the much needed
reform and democratization of the Palestinian Authority. Their stand will
not lessen the grip of religious bigotry and racism in Israeli society or reduce
the dissemination of virulent anti-Semitic propaganda in the aggrieved Arab
world. It will not stop the suicide bombers.

It simply declares: enough. Or: there is a limit. *Yesh gvul*. It provides a model
of resistance. Of disobedience. For which there will always be penalties.

None of us has yet to endure anything like what these brave conscripts are enduring, many of whom have gone to jail. To speak for peace at this moment in this country is merely to be jeered at (as in the recent Academy Awards ceremony), harassed, blacklisted (the banning by the most powerful chain of radio stations of the Dixie Chicks); in short, to be reviled as unpatriotic.

Our 'United We Stand' or 'Winner Takes All' ethos ... the United States is a country which has made patriotism equivalent to consensus. Tocqueville, still the greatest observer of the United States, remarked on an unprecedented degree of conformity in the then new country, and a hundred and seventy-five more years have only confirmed his observation.

Sometimes, given the new, radical turn in American foreign policy, it seems as if it was inevitable that the national consensus on the greatness of America, which may be activated to an extraordinary pitch of triumphalist national self-regard, was bound eventually to find expression in wars like the present one, which are assented to by a majority of the population, who have been persuaded that America has the right – even the duty – to dominate the world.

### What if the evil is unstoppable?

The usual way of heralding people who act on principle is to say that they are the vanguard of an eventually triumphant revolt against injustice.

But what if they're not? What if the evil is really unstoppable? At least in the short run. And that short run may be, is going to be, very long indeed.

My admiration for the soldiers who are resisting service in the Occupied Territories is as fierce as my belief that it will be a long time before their view prevails.

But what haunts me at this moment is acting on principle when it isn't going to alter the distribution of force, the rank injustice and murderousness of a government's policy that claims to be acting in the name not of not peace but of security.

The soldiers are there because 'we' are being attacked; or menaced. Never mind that we may have attacked them first. They are now attacking back, causing casualties. Behaving in ways that defy the 'proper' conduct of war. Behaving like 'savages', as people in our part of the world like to call people in that part of the world. And their 'savage' or 'unlawful' actions give new justification to new aggressions. And new impetus to repress or censor or persecute citizens who oppose the aggression which the government has undertaken.

Let's not underestimate the force of what we are opposing. The world is, for almost everyone, that over which we have virtually no control. Common sense and the sense of self-protectiveness tell us to accommodate to what we cannot change.

It's not hard to see how some of us might be persuaded of the justice, the necessity of a war. Especially of a war that is formulated as a small, limited military action which will actually contribute to peace or improved security; of an aggression which announces itself as a campaign of disarmament – admittedly, disarmament of the enemy, and, regrettably, requiring the application of overpowering force. An invasion which calls itself, officially, a liberation.

Never mind the disparity of forces, of wealth, of firepower, or simply of population. How many Americans know that the population of Iraq is 24 million, half of whom are children? (The population of the United States, as you will remember, is 286 million.) Not to support those who are coming under fire from the enemy seems like treason.

It may be that, in some cases, the threat is real. In such circumstances, the bearer of the moral principle seems like someone running alongside a moving train, yelling 'Stop! Stop!'

Can the train be stopped? No, it can't. At least, not now. Will other people on the train be moved to jump off and join those on the ground? Maybe some will, but most won't. (At least, not until they have a whole new panoply of fears.)

The dramaturgy of 'acting on principle' tells us that we don't have to think about whether acting on principle is expedient, or whether we can count on the eventual success of the actions we have undertaken.

Acting on principle is, we're told, a good in itself.

But it is still a political act, in the sense that you're not doing it for yourself. You don't do it just to be in the right, or to appease your own conscience; much less because you are confident your action will achieve its aim. You resist as an act of solidarity. With communities of the principled and the disobedient: here, elsewhere. In the present. In the future.

### Resistance as an act of solidarity

Thoreau's going to prison in protest against the American war on Mexico in 1849 hardly stopped the war. But the resonance of that most unpunishing and briefest spell of imprisonment (famously, a single night in jail) has not ceased to inspire principled resistance to injustice through the second half of the twentieth century and into our new era. The movement in the late 1980s to shut down the Nevada test site, a key location for the nuclear arms race, failed in its goal; the operations of the test site were unaffected by the protests. But it directly inspired the formation of a movement of protesters in far away Alma Ata who eventually succeeded in shutting down the main Soviet test site in Kazakhstan, citing the Nevada antinuclear activists as their inspiration and expressing solidarity with the Native Americans on whose land the Nevada test site had been located.

The likelihood that your acts of resistance cannot stop the injustice does not exempt you from acting in what you sincerely and reflectively hold to be the best interests of your community.

Thus: it is not in the best interests of Israel to be an oppressor.

Thus: it is not in the best interests of the United States to be a hyperpower, capable of imposing its will on any country in the world, as it chooses.

What is in the true interests of a modern community is justice. It cannot be right to systematically oppress and confine a neighbouring people. It is surely false to think that murder, expulsion, annexations, the building of walls – all that has contributed to reducing a whole people to dependence, penury, and despair – will bring security and peace to the oppressors.

It cannot be right that a president of the United States seems to believe that he has a mandate to be president of the planet, and announces that those who are not with America are with 'the terrorists.'

Those brave Israeli Jews who, in fervent and active opposition to the policies of the present government of their country, have spoken up on behalf of the plight and the rights of Palestinians, are defending the true interests of Israel. Those of us who are opposed to the plans of the present government of the United States for global hegemony are patriots speaking for the best interests of the United States.

Beyond these struggles, which are worthy of our passionate adherence, it is important to remember that in programmes of political resistance the relation of cause and effect is convoluted, and often indirect. All struggle, all resistance is – must be – concrete. And all struggle has a global resonance.

If not here, then there. If not now, then soon: elsewhere as well as here.

To Archbishop Oscar Arnulfo Romero.

To Rachel Corrie.

And to Ishai Menuchin and his comrades.

Thank you.

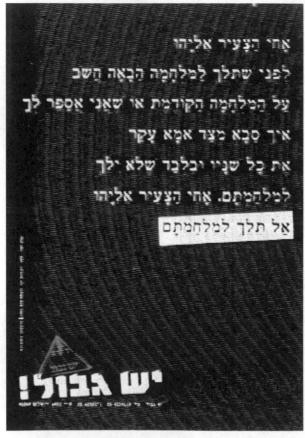

The Hebrew text of Yitzhak Laor's refusenik poem, 'My brother Eliyahu', reproduced on a Yesh Gvul poster and widely distributed in the 1980s.

# DON'T GO TO THEIR WAR*

## Yitzhak Laor

My young brother Eliyahu
Before you go off to the next war, think of
The previous war or let me tell you
How Grandfather on Mom's side pulled out
All his teeth, anything so as not to go to
Their war. My young brother Eliyahu, don't
Go to their war.

* Published 1978

# OCCUPATION MEANS MURDER

## A letter to the editor*
### Yeshayahu Leibovitz

*Professor Yeshayahu Leibovitz was an eminent Israeli scholar and academic who offered consistent moral support to the refusal movement until his death in 1994. Many refuseniks continue to hold him up as their spiritual mentor.*

Prompted by the bloodshed in the occupied territories – perpetrated by the IDF [Israel Defence Forces] at the behest of the political and military rulers of the state of Israel 25 well-intentioned Jews have referred 'the IDF soldier' to the sixth of the Ten Commandments which directs, 'Thou shall not kill'.

Are they naive or just playing innocent?

Do they not know that murder is the inescapable and rational outcome of sustaining an occupation regime over another people?

Anyone who comes to terms with such a regime, even if compliance is tacit, while yet urging soldiers to refrain from committing murder, brings to mind the Talmud phrase, 'Cut off his head but don't kill him'.

Those who detest the occupation and oppression that bring about murder should urge IDF soldiers: 'Refuse to serve in the occupied territories, so that your commanders do not turn you into a murderer'.

* Published in *Ha'aretz*, 13 May 1982

Poster designed for Yesh Gvul by David Tartokov in 2002, to mark 35 years of the Israeli occupation of the West Bank and Gaza Strip, which Yesh Gvul opposes.

# ● Introduction

## Israel's Refusenik Movement

**Peretz Kidron**

In the 1967 'Six Day War', Israel occupied the West Bank and Gaza. The rights and wrongs of that war have been argued fiercely, with Israelis claiming it was self-defence, while the Arabs call it aggression. But however one views the reasons behind the occupation, the fact remains that the Palestinian population of that region has lived under Israeli military rule ever since. That rule has been repressive, effectively depriving the Palestinian population of elementary human and civic rights, with absolute power invested in an Israeli military government. That power has been exploited for large-scale confiscation of land, on which the Israeli authorities have erected Jewish settlements with the aim of perpetuating Israel's hold. Palestinian resistance to the occupation has often been violent, including acts of terrorism against Israeli civilians. Palestinians demand an end to the occupation, and the right to establish a state of their own.

Many Israelis are opposed to the occupation, on moral and political grounds, arguing that Israel will never know peace as long as it attempts to exercise control over an alien population struggling for its national rights. Out of their opposition to the occupation, hundreds of Israeli soldiers and reservists have refused to serve in the occupied territories. Their defiance has landed many of these 'refuseniks' terms in military jails, but the refusal movement is growing and now numbers over a thousand.

This book will try to tell the story of the refuseniks.

1

## 'The Black Flag of Illegality'

On 29 October 1956, between 5 and 6 o'clock in the evening, Israeli Border Guards killed 47 people from the Palestinian village of Kafr Qasem. The villagers were returning home from work in the fields and didn't know their village had been placed under curfew by the Israeli army. The judges who composed the verdict on the soldiers responsible for the Kafr Qasem massacre coined a now famous description of orders that should not be obeyed, saying 'the black flag of illegality' flies over them. This illegality, they said, 'rescinds the soldier's duty to obey and charges him with criminal accountability for his actions'. 'The black flag of illegality' has become a central concept for the refusenik movement.

By the summer of 2003, well over a thousand Israelis of military age had declared they would refuse to take part in the army's ongoing campaign of repression against the Palestinian population. Of that number, over 500 had already rejected orders to serve in the occupied territories. In addition, a further 600 were formally committed to refuse if and when they are posted. This widespread defiance has not gone unpunished. Since the beginning of the current *intifada*, in September 2000, some 200 soldiers and officers – conscripts or reservists – have served prison terms for various levels of refusal.

The ranks of the refuseniks include a number of high school graduates who, whether out of pacifism or on political grounds, have refused outright to be inducted into the army as required by law. But the overwhelming majority are older reservists exercising what has come to be known as 'selective refusal', whereby a soldier defies – on moral or political grounds – orders to take part in a specific assignment, or a certain operation, while simultaneously proclaiming his or her willingness to carry out other, more acceptable, duties. The army has only recently been eager to prove that women Refuseniks will not be exempt from prosecution because of their sex, and in November 2003, according to Gush Shalom, kept one of them behind bars for an initial 14 days.

The number of refuseniks is significant. Israel has a population of six million – one fortieth of the population of the United States, a tenth of the population of the United Kingdom, one twentieth of the population of Japan. One can only imagine the explosive political effect in the US should 40,000 American soldiers refuse orders to take part in operations in Afghanistan, or Panama, or Iraq. Or the fallout in the United Kingdom if 10,000

British soldiers had refused to take part in operations in Northern Ireland. The impact of the refusal movement transcends mere figures. A considerable number of the refuseniks are combat soldiers or officers with a fine record of distinguished service in elite units. When persons of such impeccable military credentials are prepared to risk a prison sentence because of their profound conviction that the operations against the Palestinians are immoral and, moreover, directly harmful to the national interest, their words have to be taken seriously. Both in quantity and quality, Israel's refusal movement has had a major moral and political impact.

### Early 1970s

Selective refusal has a long tradition in Israel. In the early 1970s, in what was initially a spontaneous response, individuals who were active in the peace movement reported for their annual month of duty with their reserve units, as legally required, but promptly notified their commanders they would undertake any assignment other than service in the occupied territories! The step was taken in protest over Israel's continued occupation of the Arab lands seized in the 1967 war, and the repression to which the occupation regime subjected the Palestinian population.

The first refuseniks were greeted with shocked disbelief. It was indeed a challenge to the most sanctified institution of the young state. Right from the outset, in 1948, the Israeli army had enjoyed sacrosanct status – a natural reaction to the Holocaust that befell the Jewish people in the 1940s, when unarmed European Jews had no means of defending themselves against the Nazi murderers. With those horrors fresh in the collective memory, Israel's national ethos of the fifties and sixties regarded military service as an honour and a sacred duty – soldiers were treated with enormous respect, officers concluding their military career could virtually choose any civilian job, and many who went into politics gained rapid promotion to the highest echelons of local and national government. The army was seen as the very incarnation of renewed Jewish nationhood.

Selective refusal, as an act of moral and political defiance of the military and political hierarchy, was therefore treated as sacrilege. The establishment media expressed outrage, army commanders sent refuseniks to prison, and in some cases a refusenik was disowned and ostracised by his closest family and friends.

### The army's response

However, the military hierarchy adopted a very cautious course in punishing these acts of 'insubordination'. Confidential Israel Defence Force

(IDF) directives forbade the court-martialing of refuseniks, instead requiring them to be tried by summary procedure, where the unit commander acts as judge and sentences are limited to 35 days jail at most. Such forbearance was puzzling: traditional military discipline can never condone calculated insubordination (especially – heaven help us! – when defiance is sustained by 'seditious' political or moral conviction). Indeed, some IDF generals favoured the more draconian course of trying a select handful of refuseniks by court martial, where they would incur a sentence running into months or years. Making an example of a few would smash the refusal movement, or so the hardliners hoped.

But more prudent counsel prevailed, bowing to the fact that while court martial procedure offers greater scope for punishment, it also grants a defendant far broader rights, including the service of an attorney and the right to summon witnesses. The IDF consistently funked a confrontation, the generals having good cause to avoid facing a defence attorney who would justify his client's insubordination on the grounds that his orders – whether to invade Lebanon or suppress the Palestinian uprising – were flagrantly illegal under Israeli and international law. It is an argument that Israeli leaders, civilian and military alike, were desperate to avoid, and for many years no refusenik ever faced court-martial!

In 2003 however, on being confronted with a new and unfamiliar form of refusal, the army departed from its traditional policy. A year previously, a letter sent to prime minister Ariel Sharon by a group of high school students awaiting induction declared that they would refuse to enlist in the 'army of occupation'. When the first of over 300 signatories were summoned to induction centres for their compulsory three-year service, they lived up to their promise and refused to don uniform. Successive disciplinary jailings failed to break the youngsters' spirits; the military command then decided to court-martial six of the group's leaders. At the same time, however, other refuseniks, whether reservists or conscripts, continued to receive routine disciplinary penalties.

### Yesh Gvul – 'there's a limit'

In the early days of protest refusals, there was some public debate on the issue, but in the absence of organised support, individual acts of refusal were little more than a quixotic, private gesture with little political significance and unable to spark a broad movement. Indeed, many left-wingers continued to discharge their reserve duties in the territories, though in great moral and political distress.

But in June 1982 came the invasion of Lebanon, at the behest of then prime minister Menachem Begin and his minister of defence, General Ariel Sharon. And many a reservist who had wrestled with his conscience over his annual service in the occupied Palestinian territories now found himself in a redoubled dilemma when he was required to take part in an aggressive campaign against a neighbouring state. This was just 'Too much!', or, in colloquial Hebrew, 'Yesh Gvul' – there's a limit! And that is how Yesh Gvul was formed, with selective refusal as its *raison d'être* and driving force.

Yesh Gvul launched its campaign by sponsoring a petition by reservists objecting to service in Lebanon. After collecting over 3000 signatures to the petition, the group soon expanded its work to a wide range of activities. Whenever a refusenik was jailed, Yesh Gvul provided moral and material assistance, publicising his protest, extending financial aid to his family and dependents, holding vigils outside the prison and organising a worldwide support network, while volunteers mounted high-profile protests to challenge the Begin-Sharon government and the bloody Lebanon campaign.

With the backing of Yesh Gvul, selective refusal now became the focus, the catalyst, indeed the cutting edge of the Israeli peace movement. 168 soldiers were jailed, some repeatedly, for refusing to serve in Lebanon, and each imprisonment – immediately publicised to the maximum by Yesh Gvul – further fuelled anti-war sentiment. Yesh Gvul pursued its education-for-peace campaign with intensive leafleting aimed at soldiers at military transportation centres. Yesh Gvul has never been the largest of the Israeli peace movements, but as the mouthpiece of individuals prepared to go to prison to uphold their convictions, the group carries moral and political weight out of all proportion to its size, giving enormous impetus to the broader peace coalition.

The refusal movement is also unique in having a two-pronged effect, swaying public opinion and decision-makers alike. On top of galvanizing the anti-war movement in the streets during the Lebanon campaign, refuseniks also had a direct impact on governmental deliberations. As soldiers in increasing numbers stood up for their principles, the army abruptly ceased to be the blindly obedient 'military machine' so beloved of politicians. Instead, the military-political establishment had to reckon with soldiers who were subjecting their orders to thoughtful scrutiny, citizens-in-uniform who brought their moral and political principles to their military duties and didn't simply do whatever they were told.

## Selective refusal

In part, selective refusal is a reflection of the Jewish experience at the hands of soldiers who were 'just obeying orders'. That bitter historical lesson, translated into courageous defiance – often by the sons of Jews who had survived the European Holocaust – became a factor to be taken into account in official conference chambers. Political leaders in every country like to see their army as an obedient military machine geared to disciplined implementation of instructions from above. The abrupt change brought about by soldiers who scrutinised their orders and dared to challenge their legitimacy was not lost on Israel's political and military establishment. In 1984, after two years of bitter fighting, Israel's military leadership recommended abandoning the Lebanon campaign. On the public testimony of Major General Moshe Levy, then IDF chief of staff, one reason for the recommendation was apprehension among senior officers that refusals, then already running into the hundreds, 'would grow into thousands and tens of thousands' if the campaign went on. Levy's acknowledgement was a remarkable testimonial to the efficacy of the refusal movement.

Some years later, nationalist prime minister Benyamin Netanyahu, called to account by hardline followers over some token concessions to the Palestinians, defended his actions by arguing that, without a semblance of peace efforts by the Israeli government, any future conflict would find 'half the army refusing to fight'. He did not specify Yesh Gvul, but his listeners were left in no doubt that he was referring to the refusal movement. Further acknowledgement of the effect Yesh Gvul was having came when the group was placed under close surveillance by the Shabak security police, which, however, turned up no indictable activity.

## The first intifada

Yesh Gvul stepped up its activities with the onset of the first Palestinian *intifada* (December 1987), in the course of which some 200 soldiers went to jail for refusing to take part in the campaign of repression. In fact, instances of refusal were much more numerous – in time, many commanding officers simply gave up their attempt to discipline soldiers who refused to take part in anti-Palestinian actions in the occupied territories, instead offering them alternative duties inside pre-1967 Israel. This time too the political impact of refusal was evident, when it became a major element in the domestic pressure that ultimately forced the Shamir government to attend the 1992 Madrid peace conference – the first time official Israel consented to face-to-face talks with Palestinian representatives.

## The second intifada

Since then, Yesh Gvul has kept up its campaign to end the occupation and achieve an equitable peace between Israelis and Palestinians. In the second, *intifada al-Aqsa*, which erupted in September 2000, the group has faced an uphill task, because an overwhelming majority of Israeli opinion supports the campaign of repression against the Palestinians. In part, this public mood must be blamed on former prime minister Ehud Barak and the leadership of the Labour party, who successfully convinced Israelis that Israel had made the Palestinians a very fair peace offer, which was rejected, and the Palestinians then resorted to violence and terrorism.

In February 2001, despite an appalling record as warmonger, Ariel Sharon was elected prime minister with 63 per cent of the vote. A major factor in swinging opinion behind the hardliners were Palestinian acts of wholesale violence. Indiscriminate attacks on civilians – equally in the occupied territories and within pre-1967 Israel – convinced Jewish opinion that 'the Arabs want to kill us all', and that Israel was therefore engaged, not in a campaign of repression to cling to the territories and the illegal Jewish settlements created there, but rather in a battle for sheer physical survival. Unlike the Lebanon campaign, acknowledged by then prime minister Begin to be a 'war of choice', this time most Israelis were convinced they were engaged in a 'war of no-choice', entirely justifiable as self-defence against a murderous foe, and gave knee-jerk approval to virtually any action against the Palestinians.

In the climate of war hysteria whipped up by the media, Yesh Gvul and the refusal movement has had to cope with enormous enmity. With the general perception that 'Israel's Jews are fighting for sheer survival!', refuseniks have been denounced as traitors for refusing to take part in the so-called 'defensive campaign'. Along with the rest of the peace movement, Yesh Gvul has had the thankless task of proving conclusively that the army is being used to terrorise the Palestinians into submission, and that bloodshed on both sides is brought on by the continuing occupation.

## Denounced as traitors

Army and political leaders, abetted by establishment journalists, launched an unscrupulous campaign of denigration against the refuseniks, accusing them of betraying the national interest. But Yesh Gvul has rejected the charges, arguing that the refuseniks are actually protecting the army from the corruption of misuse by unscrupulous nationalist fanatics. In Algeria, Vietnam, Afghanistan – to give just a few examples – armies given the impossible task of subduing a rebellious civilian population were soon thoroughly demoralised as officers and soldiers were torn between committing human rights abuses and rebelling. Yesh Gvul seeks to defend the IDF from such a fate by pressing for an immediate end to the occupation. In pursuing its vigorous campaign for a peaceful solution to the Israeli-Palestinian conflict, Yesh Gvul is also working to preserve the army and confine it to its legitimate defensive role. But above all, the group is committed to doing its utmost to end the conflict with the Palestinians and achieve a just and enduring peace.

# I CANNOT TAKE PART IN YOUR CRIMES

## A letter to the Defence Minister of Israel

### by Sergio Yahni

*Sergio Yahni, who is co-director of the Alternative Information Centre and a longstanding activist with Yesh Gvul, endured three prison terms for his refusal to serve in the occupied territories during the first intifada. Now he refuses to do reserve duty in any capacity in the IDF as long as the occupation is in force. On 19 March 2002 he was sentenced to 28 days imprisonment. After he had been sentenced, Yahni addressed this eloquent letter to then defence minister Benyamin Ben Eliezer.*

An officer for whom you are responsible has sentenced me today to 28 days in military prison for my refusal to serve in reserve duty. I did not refuse only to serve in the occupied Palestinian territories, as I have for the past 15 years; I refused to serve in the Israeli army in any capacity whatsoever.

Since 29 September 2000, the Israeli army has waged a 'dirty war' against the Palestinian Authority. This dirty war includes extra-judicial killings, the murder of women and children, destruction of the economic and social infrastructure of the Palestinian population, the burning of agricultural fields and the uprooting of trees. You have sown fear and despair but failed to achieve your ultimate objective; the Palestinian people did not give up their dream of sovereignty and independence. Neither did you provide security for your own people despite all the destructive violence of the army for which you bear responsibility.

In light of your great failure, we are now witness to an intellectual debate amongst Israelis of the worst kind: a discussion about the possible deportation and the mass killing of Palestinians. The failed attempt of leaders of the Labour Party to impose a settlement on the Palestinian people has dragged us into a 'dirty war' for which

Palestinians and Israelis are paying with their lives. The racist violence of the Israeli security establishment, who do not see people but only 'terrorists', has deepened the vicious cycle of violence for both Palestinians and Israelis.

Israelis are also the victims of this war. They are the victims of the irresponsible and failed aggression of the army for which you are responsible. Even when you waged the most deadly attacks on the Palestinian people, you did not fulfill your duty: granting security to the citizens of Israel. Tanks in Ramallah cannot stop your most monstrous creation: the desperation which explodes in coffee shops. You, and the military officers under your command, have created human beings whose humanity disappears out of desperation and humiliation. You have created this despair and you cannot stop it.

It is evident to me that you have risked all of our lives solely in order to continue building illegal and immoral settlements, for the sake of Gush Etzion, Efrat and Kedumim: on behalf of the cancer which eats away at the Israeli social body. For the past 35 years, the settlements have turned Israeli society into a danger zone. The Israeli state has sown despair and death for both Palestinians and Israelis.

Therefore I will not serve in your army. Your army that calls itself the 'Israel Defense Forces', is nothing more than the armed wing of the settlement movement. This army does not exist to bring security to the citizens of Israel; it exists to guarantee the continuation of the theft of Palestinian land. As a Jew, I am repelled by the crimes this militia commits against the Palestinian people.

It is both my Jewish and human duty to resolutely refuse to take any part in this army. As the son of a people victim to pogroms and destruction, I cannot be a part of your insane policies. As a human being, it is my duty to refuse to participate in any institution which commits crimes against humanity.

# The Early Refuseniks

## Balance*

**by Yitzhak Laor**

*In December 1972, Yitzhak Laor – at the time a literature student at Tel Aviv University – was one of the first two IDF reservists to declare their 'selective refusal' to serve in the occupied territories, for which they incurred terms in a military prison. Their unprecedented refusal was a sensation at the time, prompting vigorous condemnation from most sections of Israeli opinion. Laor has since gone on to achieve renown in Israel as a leading poet, novelist and literary critic.*

The gunner who rubbed out a hospital the pilot
Who burned a refugee camp the journalist
Who wooed hearts and minds for murder the actor
Who turned the whole thing into just one more war the teacher
Who sanctioned the bloodshed in class the rabbi
Who sanctified the killings the minister
Who raised a sweaty arm in favour the paratrooper
Who shot the third-time refugee the poet
Who lauded the nation on its finest hour and the nation
Who scented blood and blessed the Mig. The even-handed
Who said let's wait and see the party hack
Who went out of his way to flatter the army the sales clerk
Who scented traitors the policeman
Who beat an Arab in the anxious street the officer
Who was scared of refusing the prime minister
Who gulped down the blood eagerly. They shall not be cleansed.

* From *Poems 1974–1992*, Kibbutz Hameuhad Publishing House, 2002. 'Balance' was written in 1982.

Yesh Gvul chairperson Ishai Menuchin broadcasts a message of encouragement to jailed refuseniks at one of the regular monthly vigils held on Mount Carmel, overlooking the military prison at Atlit.

# Saying 'no' loudly and clearly

## by Ishai Menuchin

*Ishai Menuchin is the chairperson of Yesh Gvul, of which he was a co-founder in 1982. An IDF reserve major, he served a term in military jail in February–March 1983 for refusal to serve in Lebanon. Born 1958, in Rehovot, Menuchin lives near Jerusalem with his wife Dina, and their three children. He holds a Hebrew University master's degree in cognitive psychology, and is writing his Ph.D. thesis on 'Justification, pluralism and civil disobedience'. On top of writing and editing dozens of Yesh Gvul pamphlets and booklets for distribution to soldiers, Menuchin also promoted and edited the anthology* Democracy and Obedience *on the law and limits of obedience in a democratic society, with essays by leading Israeli and foreign philosophers, legal experts and writers, including one by Menuchin himself. Together with Dina Menuchin, he also edited* Limits of Obedience, *developing the subject of compliance and democracy in relation to the Lebanon war; contributors include Noam Chomsky and Prof. Yeshayahu Leibovitz.*

Twenty years ago, when I was first inducted into the army, to serve as paratrooper and officer for four and half years, I took an oath to defend my country and obey my commanders. I was young, a patriot, probably naive, and sure that as a soldier I would only defend my home and country. It never occurred to me that I might be used as a tool of occupation or be asked to fight in wars of choice, as opposed to wars of defence. It took me one war, the Lebanon war, many dead friends, and some periods of service in the occupied territories to find that I was wrong, whereupon I refused to partake further in acts of occupation, spending 35 days in military prison as a consequence.

Being a citizen in a democracy carries with it a commitment to democratic values and a responsibility for your actions. It is morally impossible to be both a devoted democratic citizen and a regular offender against democratic values, and it is equally impossible to be such a citizen and neglect your democratic responsibility for your actions. Depriving people of the right to equality and freedom, and keeping them under occupation, is by definition an anti-democratic act. Keeping more than three and a half million Palestinians under brutal occupation for so many years is anti-democratic conduct that drives me, and hundreds of thousands of Israeli citizens, to oppose our government's policies and the army's actions in the territories.

על דמוקרטיה וציות

The front cover of *Democracy and Obedience*, a collection of essays edited by Ishai Menuchin, and published in March 1990.

My commitment to democratic values, and my responsibility for my actions, brought me to act against the occupation – to sign petitions, write ads, take part in demonstrations and vigils etc. But all these acts of opposition were not enough when I was required to participate – and in my capacity as officer, to order others to do likewise – in the occupation and its evils. I decided to selectively refuse military orders, if they included my presence in the territories. I will continue to serve in the Israeli Defense Force, but not in the Israeli Occupation Force. I will not obey 'illegal' orders to execute potential terrorists, or fire into civilian demonstrations. (Since October 2000 close on 3,000 Palestinians have been killed by my army, including a significant number of children and minors, and an equally striking number executed). In addition, I will not take part in 'less violent' actions such as keeping Palestinians under curfew for months, manning roadblocks that prevent civilians moving from town to town, or participating in house demolitions and any other acts of repression in the Palestinian territories.

However, it is not enough for me personally to take no part in all these immoral acts, keeping my hands clean while my fellow citizens keep the Palestinians under occupation and rob them of their basic human rights. This too seems to me immoral and offends my commitment to democratic values. I believe in raised awareness of selective refusal as an option and as a political statement.

Hearing more and more hard testimony about massive violations of Palestinian human rights, it is increasingly evident that it is my right and duty as a citizen to say 'No' in the clearest and most overt fashion.

I refuse to take part in the occupation because I am an Israeli citizen – and take this citizenship seriously. I am not alone. Well over a thousand Israelis have declared that they will defend Israel, but will take no further part in the occupation. Since the onset of the second *intifada*, two hundred of these devoted Israeli citizens have been imprisoned for their commitment to these values. Our refusal to take part in these actions is a model for other Israelis, illustrating that there is an alternative to participation in occupation.

## Bring the soldiers home!

*In protest over Israel's invasion of Lebanon in June 1982, Yesh Gvul sponsored a petition that was signed by over 3000 reservists in 1982–3. This is what it said:*

We have sworn to defend the wellbeing and security of the state of Israel. We are faithful to that oath. Therefore we appeal to be allowed to render our reserve service within the boundaries of the state of Israel, and not on Lebanese soil.

## An artist at Ansar

### by Zvi Goldstein

*Zvi Goldstein, artist and art teacher at Jerusalem's Bezalel art academy, was jailed for refusal to serve in Lebanon.*

In view of the storm my case has provoked, I feel obliged to explain the reasons that induced me to refuse to serve in Lebanon.

Although I was one of the signatories of the Yesh Gvul petition requesting release from service in Lebanon, I did not venture to express my objections in a practical manner until I was summoned to serve at the Ansar detention camp [that housed Palestinians and Lebanese detained without trial by the Israeli forces]. Ansar contrived to arouse in me both my political and civic feelings, and my artistic sensitivity to images.

Anselm Kipfer, the contemporary German artist, employs mythological tools to analyse his people's history. An Israeli Kipfer would probably resort to two images to comprehend our history: the Western Wall [a sanctified Jewish site in Jerusalem, sole relic of the Temple destroyed by the Romans 2000 years ago], and the Ansar detention camp, symbol of our 'enlightened' occupation of Lebanon, and man's domination by man.

I am not calling upon anyone to take a similar step. With that, we are obliged not merely to acknowledge mentally that we adhere to something; we should also give visual expression to our views.

Whatsoever we are unable to express today as human beings, we will be unable to express tomorrow as artists and intellectuals. I was fortunate that, due to the efforts of Yesh Gvul, my case was brought to the attention of the artistic community in Israel. But there are others who were imprisoned, and remain incarcerated for longer periods, anonymously and alone with their consciences.

## Discovering the Palestinians

### by Mike Levine

*Scion of a prominent right-wing family, Mike Levine was imprisoned for refusal during the 1982–4 Lebanon campaign, going on to become an activist with Yesh Gvul and serving as the group's spokesperson. He is currently head of the trade union committee at the transport ministry.*

I grew up in a very political home where there was total adulation of Zeev Jabotinsky [the right-wing Zionist writer, philosopher and ideologue], side by side with hatred of the Labour Party. My father had been an active Zionist in Russia and was imprisoned there several times. On arrival in this country he became a leading member of the nationalist Revisionist party. My upbringing was nationalist, but very liberal, with no trace of racism. True, my parents totally ignored Palestinian national aspirations, but I wasn't taught to hate them. In 1950, my father was elected to the Knesset for the right-wing Herut party.

My mother too was politically conscious and greatly involved in the Revisionist movement. She was Jabotinsky's secretary. Up to age 14, I was a member of Betar, the Revisionist youth movement. At my school in north

Tel Aviv I was regarded as a right-wing extremist, one of three in the whole school.

I began to change after the 1967 war, while studying at the Jerusalem Hebrew University. I began to attend left-wing events, and for the first time I learned about the Palestinian national problem. I had been brought up with the knowledge of one side only, the Jewish side; suddenly I discovered we have partners in this land, with demands of their own.

That was the beginning of my 'downfall'. As a member of Herut, you have to be totally loyal to the movement and its members. In the 1969 elections I cast a blank ballot, finding it hard to vote against the party of my youth.

My father had died before my 'downfall', but I had bitter arguments with my mother. She was an enlightened, liberal woman, but she couldn't accept that there is a Palestinian people with rights of its own in this country. It demolished her whole value system

My first thoughts of refusal came up during the Lebanon war. First time I was called up, I reported for duty. The second time I refused and joined Yesh Gvul. I should stress that my activity in the movement is in no way directed against the state of Israel. I do it out of concern and dread over what is happening here. I believe my refusal is an act of personal protest stemming from unwillingness to take part in the brutal acts committed by the Israeli army. Furthermore, I consider my refusal to be a patriotic act. I am entirely at peace with my convictions, I continue to be a member of the nationalist health insurance fund and continue to support the Jerusalem Betar football team, the emblem of the right-wing movement.

## In solidarity with the almond trees

### by Peretz Kidron

Reaching the top of the slope, we halted briefly to catch our breath. It was heavy going over the soft sands of Sinai, with our Bedouin tracker setting a brisk pace that had us, chubby reservists well beyond the flush of youth, and encumbered by rifles and combat webbing, panting heavily in the desert heat.

Wiping the sweat from my face, I heard the roar of a machine and my eyes were drawn to a scene of intensive activity. Beyond the rolling dunes, a bulldozer was at work, engine whining as its heavy blade churned the light soil. Before my stunned gaze, the driver set it in forward gear to lunge at a tree, bending it to the ground before uprooting it bodily. To his rear lay a long line of ravaged trunks the mechanical monster had already torn up, and the remaining trees stood waiting to undergo the same fate. Rows of almond trees.

It was a startling sight. Israel of those days was renowned worldwide for 'conquering the desert and converting it into a flourishing garden', and here was a flourishing grove of fruit trees being systematically reduced to bare desert. It was painful to see human endeavour demolished by human intent. 'What's that?', I asked the tracker. He cast a casual gaze at the machine. 'They're clearing the ground for a new Jewish settlement,' he said offhandedly. He need say no more.

It was 1974, seven years after Israel's conquest of the Sinai peninsula, and the government of the day was intent on strengthening its grip on the occupied peninsula by planting Israeli settlers at strategic points, displacing the region's Arab population. I knew all about the colonisation drive from media reports, and I was among the as-yet small band of anti-occupation campaigners who responded with vigorous but hitherto ineffective protest actions. But abstract knowledge was one thing: witnessing the process with my own eyes made it painful and inescapable.

That evening, back in our tent, somebody switched on a transistor radio to pick up the news. The main headlines were followed by a smaller item: 'Israeli military authorities in Sinai have taken action against Bedouin squatters who illegally seized state land in recent months. The squatters tried to lay claim to the land by planting almond saplings as proof of ownership. The saplings have been removed.'

That barefaced lie hit me like a physical blow in the face. My years in the kibbutz had set me tending in the fruit groves, and I knew something about trees. Nobody could convince me that trees whose uprooting required such effort by the powerful bulldozer were newly planted saplings! They were mature, well-rooted trees, and to reach that size in the inhospitable desert, they must have enjoyed loving care for many years, several decades at least. So the Bedouin families living there were long-time residents, not 'squatter' newcomers! On top of all its other sins and iniquities, my government was covering up its misdeeds in the occupied territories by resorting to deliberate untruths.

My annual military reserve service had long been engaging my conscience. Each time I reported with my unit, I shuddered at the prospect of being sent into some area of the occupied territories. I am no pacifist. I had completed my regular conscript service, I routinely did armed guard duty at the kibbutz and I was ready to defend my country against external aggression. But policing occupied Arab territory could not be regarded as 'defending my country'. I knew that the duties I would discharge – however reluctantly – were my own small contribution towards perpetuating Israel's domination of other people and their land. True, I was not alone: thousands of soldiers, conscripts and reservists alike, were pursuing similar assignments on a daily basis. The 'Israel Defence Force' (IDF) was rapidly turning into the IOF – Israel *Occupation* Force.

And to my dismay, I was part of it. It was an irritating awareness, in flat contradiction to my own deepest convictions, to my total commitment to the anti-occupation campaign. It was a strange predicament: I spent eleven months of the year campaigning against the occupation, and the twelfth month enforcing it! But what could I do? Disobey orders?

The notion of disobedience was not alien to me. Several personal friends and colleagues had refused to serve in the territories, thereby incurring jail sentences and widespread condemnation. Reserve duty was both a legal obligation and a socially enforced norm. This was an era when the army was sacrosanct, evasion of service was rare, and malingerers who sought pretexts to evade it were frowned upon. Conscious politically motivated refusal – insofar as it existed at all – was regarded as sacrilege, disloyalty, a stab in the back.

I was unreservedly in favour of refusal. As for myself, I could perhaps face up to the social consequences of such a protest, my immediate circle largely sharing my own views. But I had to consider my two teenaged children, growing up in a border kibbutz with a firm military tradition. Did I have the right to expose them to sneers over a father who evaded his national security duties?

The issue had haunted me ever since two close friends had publicly refused service in the territories, and I found myself unable to express my solidarity in anything more useful than smearing an unoffending marble wall at Tel Aviv University with foot-high slogans demanding their release. I felt ashamed at my failure to emulate their bold act, but equally I hesitated at the consequences. I remained undecided, torn between conviction and apprehension.

It was in this ambivalent mood that I had reported for service once more, to find myself again posted to Sinai. As ever, I went about my duties half-heartedly, venting my frustrations after my watch by indulging in raucous political arguments with the right-wingers with whom I shared a tent. It passed the time but did little to resolve my soul-searching.

Finally, it was that row of ravaged almond trees – and the lies conveyed in the fruity tones of the radio announcer – that tilted the balance for me.

My mind was made up. It was bizarre: I consider myself above all a humanist, concerned for my fellow human beings. But what spurred me to take action was not the mistreatment of a flesh-and-blood person: my outrage took fire over the abuse of a fruit grove. In time, I was to learn that this was not exceptional: other refuseniks told me they too had been moved to defiance by some ostensibly trivial, undramatic incident.

The die was cast. Next time I was called in for reserve duty, I wrote to my unit in advance to declare that 'as a matter of conscience and conviction, I refuse to serve in the occupied territories'. There was no response, but on reporting for duty I lost no time in notifying my officers that I refused 'to cross the green line in uniform'. To my surprise (and perhaps, disappointment) the dire consequences I had foreseen failed to materialise. After the initial looks of amazement and some half-hearted attempts to bully me into compliance, I was seconded to assignments inside pre-1967 Israel. The pattern repeated itself whenever I was summoned to service. My resistance evoked alternate doses of cajoling with threats of punishment and court martial, but the blustering came to nothing. It was a strange paradox: my officers were all without exception extreme right-wingers. Perhaps precisely for that reason, my protest seemed to evoke their grudging respect. Be that as it may, I was never jailed, in spite of my persistent and reiterated refusal.

But although overcoming my misgivings, I accomplished little. Above all, my frustration stemmed from the fact that the protest went almost entirely unnoticed. Beyond my immediate circle of acquaintances – and of course, the other reservists in my unit – nobody so much as knew of my refusal. In the absence of an organised refusal movement, there would have been nobody to take up my case even if I had gone to jail.

Under the circumstances, my acts of refusal were little more than quixotic gestures. But at the very least, my conscience was at peace, and I could regard myself in the mirror without shame. And in time, individual acts like mine percolated into the thinking of the radical peace movement. Eight years after I reached my own private decision, the banner of refusal was taken up by a group of younger reservists who proclaimed that they had reached the limits of obedience. In Hebrew: 'Yesh Gvul!' First chance I got, I joined.

# General, your tank is a powerful vehicle

*Among its earliest publications, Yesh Gvul printed a poster with the Hebrew translation of this famous poem by German anti-Nazi playwright and poet Bertolt Brecht. The poem, conveying the essence of the refusenik's philosophy with its call for a thinking soldier, has become the unofficial credo of Yesh Gvul.*

General, your tank is a powerful vehicle
It tramples the forest, it crushes a hundred men.
But it has one flaw:
It requires a driver.

General, your bomber is strong.
It flies faster than the storm, it louds more than an elephant.
But it has one flaw:
It requires a mechanic.

General, man is very useful.
He knows how to fly, he knows how to murder.
But he has one flaw;
He knows how to think.

Poster issued by Yesh Gvul in 1988, during the first intifada. The headline says, 'Daddy, what are you doing in the occupied territories?'

# The First *Intifada*

The first *intifada* erupted in December 1987, when the Palestinian population, exasperated beyond further endurance by twenty years of occupation, launched massive protests that soon turned into violent confrontations with Israeli troops. A brutal campaign of repression was conducted under the leadership of then defence minister Yitzhak Rabin, who instructed his military commanders to 'break the arms and legs' of Palestinian protesters. Outrage over revelations of widespread human rights violations arising from this directive prompted a renewed wave of refusals, and close on 200 IDF refuseniks were jailed in the course of the *intifada*. In fact, the actual number of refusals was far in excess of that figure.

Yesh Gvul stepped up its campaign against the occupation. Ignoring surveillance by the Shabak security police, the group organised vigils, protests, and the widespread leafletting of military transportation centres in an effort to educate soldiers about the moral and legal responsibility they bear for their actions. The message got through, and many military units witnessed impassioned arguments around the refusal issue.

## I'm no martyr
### by Hanoch Livneh

*Hanoch Livneh was jailed for refusal in October 1988. Married with two daughters, a bank employee and head of the employees' trade union committee, Livneh was a longtime activist with Yesh Gvul, serving as the group's spokesperson. He remains active in politics and the bank employees' trade union.*

Many days, nights mainly, I spent soul-searching before coming to my decision to refuse, which is so far-reaching and therefore so difficult. The small number of refuseniks jailed so far also seems to indicate that 'the majority is in the right'. I'm no martyr, and I need to go to prison like I need a hole in the head. But if I get called up and I'm sent to the Gaza Strip, I'd choke, simply choke. That impossible march, once or twice a year, with helmet and club, infiltrates the national and nationalist mechanism.

What will I take with me when I leave prison? I'll be able to tell my daughters: 'That isn't me, that soldier you see on television'. What good will that do me? The fact that I'm in the right? The fact it won't be me that's condemned by history and justice; instead it will be those who wanted to send me to inflict bruises and break bones and poke my filthy club into the pus of another people? Will I find comfort in the fact that everybody will tell me I was in the right? I doubt it. But there's no other choice left to me.

## Whatever the price

### Rami Hasson

*Scion of a Sephardi Jewish family that has lived in Jerusalem for 28 generations, Hasson worked for 9 years as instructor for delinquent youth before going on to run a health club. As a reservist, he served as corporal with the engineer corps. He refused a posting to serve as guard at the notorious Fara detention camp housing Palestinians interned during the* intifada. *Possibly because of his family's strong right-wing links, Hasson was picked out for repeated imprisonments. First jailed in May 1988, he went on to a total of 146 days in jail – 5 consecutive sentences that threatened to destroy his business – but he did not relent. His victimisation became a* cause célèbre. *Ultimately, a public campaign by Yesh Gvul forced the army to halt its persecution of him.*

It does not so much as occur to me to evade service by having my medical category downgraded or taking a trip abroad. I simply wish to render my service without being required to engage in repression, and any service in the West Bank or Gaza nowadays entails frightful repression. We're told we pay a light price compared to draft resisters in the United States; that may be true, but I regard it as an enormous price, not the least being the financial burden of forfeiting military pay through my imprisonment. I hope I can stand up to the threats of repeated imprisonment. I'm simply unwilling to serve there whatever the price.

Jerusalem health spa director, Rami Hasson, as he appeared in the Events section of *Kol Ha'ir*, a Jerusalem weekly, during the first *intifada*. His placard reads, 'A visit to encourage refuseniks jailed at Military Prison 6 to be held on the second day of the Jewish New Year (Friday September 29). Transport from Binyaney Ha'Umma at 11.00'.

# The problem is in Jewish society

## by Menahem Hefetz

*Born in 1961 to parents who immigrated respectively from Iraq and Russia, Menahem Hefetz was a maths teacher and a student at Tel Aviv University in 1988 when he was jailed for refusal to serve in the occupied territories.*

I became aware of the Jewish-Palestinian problem while still at school. When I was 17, I and some classmates wrote to prime minister Menachem Begin demanding his personal action to get us out of the occupied territories as quickly as possible, adding that he would bear the responsibility for the next war.

I was completing my compulsory military service in June 1982 when the Lebanon war began. My release was delayed for 3 months, my battalion was sent to Lebanon and many of my friends were killed there.

Although I thought the invasion was a great mistake, I didn't refuse then. I didn't want to abandon my friends at that difficult time and, also, I feared the consequences of refusal and disobeying orders and military law.

After my release from the army, I began to help organize Re'ut, a Jewish-Arab youth movement. I've always believed that the core of the problem is in Jewish society, and the solution has to be in education and co-existence. Still fighting shy of disobeying, I did several terms of reserve duty in the occupied territories, in the Golan and Lebanon, the scenes of death coming back to haunt me.

In time, I began to sense that Jewish society doesn't want to give serious consideration to the conflict with the Palestinians, as though there were a fear of solving it. It seems much more convenient to hang everything upon 'national security', thus evading a solution and refraining from facing important internal problems.

During 1987 I toured the occupied territories, meeting intellectuals and ordinary folk. Then the *intifada* began, and by July 1988 I had made up my mind despite my hesitations. I joined Yesh Gvul and informed my commander by letter I would refuse my upcoming posting to Ramallah.

When I refused to go with the others to Ramallah, my commander left me in camp, saying I was going AWOL. I suppose they preferred to deal with me as a deserter, or traitor, rather than a loyal soldier who simply refuses to serve beyond the green line.

The colonel before whom I stood trial pressed me to reach a compromise, but I refused again and urged him to judge me according to military regulations. I got 21 days in prison. My unit no longer calls me for service in the occupied territories. I am active with Yesh Gvul and Re'ut, spending my time with Arabs in an effort to find a 'bridge over troubled waters'. But I made a clear statement to the army: 'There's a limit!'

# Refusal to collaborate
## by Dudu Palma

*A member of Kibbutz Kfar Hanassi, and father of four, Dudu Palma's parents were Holocaust survivors. During his compulsory 3-year military service up to 1970 he was a paratrooper. A graphic artist, he has also written plays, poetry and stories.*

The first time I went to prison was in 1983 – 35 days for refusing to serve in the Lebanon campaign. I had taken part in the battles in the Sidon and Beirut sectors.

My second imprisonment was for refusal to serve in the occupied territories. With the outbreak of the Lebanon war, I grasped that, if I feel responsible for the fate of democracy in this country, I can no longer share in undemocratic actions verging on war crimes.

The immediate choice I faced was either to act like a rhinoceros (the conformist image in the well-known play by Ionesco) and play along – or protest. The refusal to collaborate with the degrading occupation and its ugliest aspects seems the correct thing to do, now more than ever, so correct that it seems incredible that a people that only recently gained its own national independence now experiences such ease in denying another people a similar independence. I believe that with this step, I am defending the fragile democracy still clinging on amongst us, but being gradually swept towards the chasm by a rising tide of nationalism and Khomeinist fundamentalism.

# I am an Arab Jew

## by Meir Amor

*The son of Moroccan immigrants, Meir Amor did his military service with the Golani brigade, achieving the rank of captain. On release from the army, he studied sociology at Tel Aviv university. Concerned over the lack of opportunity for children of 'Mizrachi' (Mideastern) origin, he became active with a parents' association fostering their education. Connecting discrimination against the Mizrachi community with the occupation, he refused to serve in the occupied territories and was jailed for 21 days in February 1988 for refusal to serve as guard at Megiddo prison, where Palestinians are detained without trial. Shortly after his release, he undertook a speaking tour of North America on behalf of Yesh Gvul, together with Peretz Kidron. Amor now resides in Toronto, Canada.*

What we are asked to do in the occupied territories is what the politicians should be doing. So we selectively refuse to do the job; we throw the ball back at the politicians and tell them: it's a political problem. Find leaders of the Palestinians and deal with them.

There is no way we can avoid the existence of the Palestinians. It is of no significance if we accept their political leadership or not. They are a nation with different interests from other Arabs. When I served in Lebanon, I saw Lebanese and Syrians murder Palestinians. We have to face it. Palestinians are not Arabs, as Jews are not Israelis.

To be an Israeli, you must serve in the army. To serve in the army means to fight Arabs. So fighting Arabs means fighting for your own identity. We are Jews, not Moslems, but in Morocco my family lived with Arabs for the past 500 years. Part of my culture is Arab. Because in Israel Arabs are defined as the enemy, having any trace of Arab culture means being on the Arab side. It's contradictory.

I am an Arab Jew, I have no complexes about it. Living with Arabs was not paradise, but it was a lot better than living with Christians. Therefore we should find a way to talk to Palestinians. This is not romanticism, it's in my family life. We speak Arabic, we eat Arab food, we listen to Arab music.

I fully represent the effective integration of Mideastern (Sephardi) Jews into Israeli society. I graduated from high school and university, I served in the army and became an officer. But now I have these questions, and that's how I became a refusenik.

# Joint declaration of Yesh Gvul and Beit Sahour, 2 December 1989

*Beit Sahour is a small Palestinian town on the outskirts of Bethlehem. During the first intifada, the people of Beit Sahour adopted a strategy of non-violent civil disobedience by refusing to pay taxes to the Israeli occupation authorities. Despite enormous pressure and individual intimidation, townspeople refused to give way. Recognising this courageous course of action as a Palestinian parallel of Yesh Gvul's own form of non-violent resistance to the occupation, Yesh Gvul set up contacts with the town, with repeated solidarity visits and expressions of support. The following is a joint statement issued on 2 December 1989:*

We, members of Yesh Gvul who refuse on conscientious grounds to take a hand in the brutal acts of repression going on in the occupied territories, and residents of Beit Sahour, who adopt non-violent resistance in our campaign against the occupation, refusing to pay for the occupation apparatus, meet to hold a genuine dialogue, breaking through the deformed relationship between the Israeli and Palestinian peoples.

Dialogue is the only alternative to the bloodshed, the mass arrests and deportations, and it enfolds the hope for mutual understanding and a solution based upon agreement.

The prolonged occupation is not exclusively the problem of the Palestinian people, which seeks to give expression to its national aspirations by establishment of an independent Palestinian state alongside the state of Israel. The occupation endangers the existence of Israel as a free society based upon enlightened democratic values. No Israeli can be truly free as long as one Palestinian is subject to the oppression of occupation!

At this time of fateful political change, it is vital that we, Israelis and Palestinians, throw off the yoke of prejudice, traditions of enmity and hatred, and mould our joint future in mutual respect and openness and on the profound inner conviction that it is only a political settlement, based upon mutual recognition of the national rights of each people to live in its own independent national state, that can extricate us from the cycle of hatred and violence, and secure our joint future.

We are convinced that the future of both peoples will be secured only by peace, that the occupation is a calamity which paves the way for further war.

# Father and son: refuseniks

## Carlos and Amit Levinhoff

*Carlos Levinhoff was born in Holland in 1946, the first child to be born to Jewish survivors of the Buchenwald concentration camp. When he was 6, his parents moved to Uruguay, where he received his schooling. He married Irene Bleier, daughter of a prominent Uruguayan politician, who as senator was later arrested by the military regime in 1975 and subsequently 'disappeared' without trace. In 1967 the couple emigrated to Israel, where Carlos found work as a journalist with the Communist weekly* Zu Haderech, *Irene as a hospital nurse.*

*In February 1989, Carlos was jailed for refusal to serve in the West Bank. He completed his 35-day sentence just five days before his son Amit was imprisoned on the same charge. Amit, inducted in August 1988, was imprisoned four consecutive times during his regular 3-year conscript service, for refusing to serve in the occupied territories. Before his call up, Amit had been founder-member and spokesman for a group of 15 high school students who wrote to then defence minister Yitzhak Rabin declaring that when conscripted into the army, they wished to serve within the green line (pre-1967 Israel) 'so as not to take part in repressive actions and occupation, which is definitely against our consciences ... If ordered to take part in repressive actions, we will be obliged to refuse'. While still a teenager, Amit represented the group on Israeli TV and in interviews with foreign media.*

*Carlos Levinhoff writes:*

I didn't need the intifada to grasp that the day would come when the volcano would erupt. There's no call to be better, purer, brighter, or even saintly. You simply have to be just, balanced and sane. And that is within the power of any Israeli anywhere.

The first letter I wrote the army about refusal to serve in the territories bears the date June 1973 – a few months before the October 1973 'Yom Kippur' war. I didn't go to jail that time, and I continued to do regular reserve duty for a time, waiting for the Yom Kippur shock to wear off.

Tragically, Israeli governments have done nothing to lighten my burden, continuing their 'enlightened' occupation all the way....

It's very hard to refuse. There's the wish to be with all the others, to shoot and beat (or weep) – it's a powerful social force... But I won't go to serve the occupation as a peace-loving, internationalist mercenary. There is an alternative. Sure there is! Like all other political alternatives, it carries its risks, uncertainties and mutual suspicions.... A further war will bring absolute security – in the world to come! For the time being, let's settle for two states for two peoples, and peace will come to Israel and Palestine.

Just don't recruit the Holocaust in place of the refuseniks. The subject has been so manipulated, it's slightly awkward to mention that Auschwitz means something to me too, after my parents spent a couple of years in Nazi concentration camps. I've imbibed a sense of the camps from birth; don't brandish Auschwitz to cover up, to justify, to explain, to conceal. Such use makes the matter a boomerang, and that's unjust to those who experienced the worst of all. Don't allow Shamir, Sharon, Netanyahu, Rabin and their ilk to take the name of the Holocaust in vain.

What more can I say ? That I have a son, Israeli-born, who wears the same uniform and experiences the same dilemma. The fault isn't his but those who laid down a policy of 'not an inch', 'we shall never talk', who have on their consciences thousands of Palestinians detained, wounded, maimed and killed. At the very least I am not prepared to play their game, on a court that isn't mine, at least not in this uniform.

# Spiral of evil

## by Stephen Langfur

*Born in the US in 1941, Langfur received Conscientious Objector status during the Vietnam war. He studied at various US universities, got his Ph.D. ('Death's Second Half: A response to Heidegger's Question of the Meaning of Being through the insights of Buber and the Findings of Freud') at Syracuse University in 1977. Langfur emigrated to Israel in 1979, making his living as a tour guide. Despite his previous CO status, he consented to serve in the IDF. On 30 October 1989 he was sentenced to 21 days' detention for refusal to serve in the West Bank.*

Under what circumstances is it right for one people to govern another people without the consent of the governed?

Even when it seems to be a situation of 'Ein Breira' ['no choice'] occupation remains immoral unless the ruling people tries, with all possible speed, to create a new and better alternative. But we Israelis have dragged our feet for 27 years. The relative submissiveness of the Palestinians from 1967 to 1987 lulled us into thinking that occupation was normal. It was abnormal. When one people sits upon another, *intifada* is normal. It will go on, therefore, and with each passing year, the extremists among the Palestinians will gain in strength, while the patent immorality of occupation will isolate us from America and Western Europe. Time is against us, has been against us from the start. If ever the threat of isolation forces our hand, we shall have to give up much more than we can afford.

The basic moral law here is the Torah, as stated by the Jewish sage of antiquity, Hillel: 'What is hateful to you, do not unto others'. Its principle: another person's life is as important to him as mine is to me. Insofar as I owe my own being to other persons, that law is basic to being human. We are stuck with it. When we violate it, we feel guilt. There is, however, a way to oppress others and not feel guilt. The moral law applies to persons, so one can avoid feeling guilt by persuading oneself that the oppressed are subhuman. The doctrine of the sub-humanity of the Arabs is in full swing among us ('grasshoppers', 'cockroaches', 'one thousandth of a Jew', 'animals', 'the dirtiest people on earth'). But then, instead of guilt, one feels dread of their ultimate revenge. And because one has pushed their humanity into the unconscious, the oppressed seem not only like animals, but like animals with demoniacal properties. So one feels threatened and beats them harder, and then there is more guilt to avoid, so one de-humanizes them more, and on and on: it is the spiral of evil. One cannot sit upon another people without de-humanizing them. This is my green line. I refuse to de-humanize the Arabs.

# The limit is human life
## by David Ovadia

*David Ovadia, married with 3 children, Israeli-born to parents who immigrated from Iran, employed as an industrial electrician and active with associations for the welfare of the Mizrachi communities, was sentenced to 28 days in July 1989 for refusal to serve in the occupied territories.*

During my conscript service, I was a fervent right-winger, a supporter of Likud. During the 1973 war I drove an ambulance and saw all the terrible things that happen in wartime. At the time, it didn't abruptly change my opinions. When there was talk of a cease-fire, I was among those who objected. It took me a few years after my release from the army. The more I thought about it, the more I realised there's no point in war, lots of blood-shed and for what? Just for land and slogans.

I did some tours of reserve duty in the Sinai peninsula, then when the Lebanon campaign began I refused the first time I was sent there, but got posted to the south instead. Then one day out of the blue I was seconded to another unit and told I was going to Gaza. I refused on the spot, out of instinct. I don't see any reason to serve there. I can't do things I don't agree with.

There are things the army does that I don't like because they're inefficient and I'm crazy about efficiency. There are things the army does that you accept because that's the law. But there's a limit! That limit is human life. That's what I feel. The moment the army sends me to repress people, even if I don't actually take part in it, I won't go. They tell you all the time you shouldn't mix politics in with the army, but here too there's a limit. You can't expect a person to split his mind in two because he takes his political opinions to his military service. A man isn't a machine; I don't have a switch in my brain to turn off my thoughts.

My only difficulty is the financial one because when I go to jail for refusal I miss out on my pay. But I prefer the financial problem; I can sleep well enough in jail; it's better than serving in the territories and being unable to sleep at night.

How can you change a person's mind by jailing him? People get locked up so as not to harm others. But you can't change their political opinions in jail; on the contrary. You can *educate* or *persuade* people to change their views. Compare a deserter to a refusenik: a deserter goes to jail because he committed an offence, and he'd better not desert again. But a refusenik leaves prison and doesn't think that what he did was an offence, so he'll repeat it. Jail doesn't solve anything.

My wife agrees with me about being a refusenik; my kids are small but I don't conceal from them that I refused and got jailed for it. You can't flog a dead horse. As far as the army's concerned, a refusenik is a dead horse.

# Yom Kippur Plea for Forgiveness

*In protest over the brutal campaign of repression unleashed against the first Palestinian* intifada, *Yesh Gvul published the following as an advertisement in advance of the Jewish religious festival of Yom Kippur (Day of Atonement), when Jews make atonement and seek absolution for the sins of the past year. According to Jewish tradition, the supplication of the Yom Kippur prayers relates exclusively to sins against God. In relation to sins against his/her fellow human beings, it is up to the worshipper to apologise, and make atonement and reparation directly to the injured party. The text closely echoes one of the main Yom Kippur prayers; it is addressed to God and enumerates the sins committed (collectively) by the state of Israel.*

For the sin that we have sinned before You in repression of a people;
And for the sin that we sinned before You in killing hundreds of Palestinians, including children;
For the sin that we have sinned before You in injuring tens of thousands;
And for the sin that we have sinned before You in breaking limbs;
For the sin that we have sinned before You in administrative detention;
And for the sin that we have sinned before You in inequality before the law;
For the sin that we have sinned before You in dividing families;
For the sin that we have sinned before You in adulating the soil;
And for the sin that we have sinned before You in demeaning the human likeness, theirs and ours;
For the sin that we have sinned before You in corrupting the souls of young soldiers;
And for the sin that we have sinned before You by justifying our deeds with the argument that 'there's no other choice';
For the sin that we have sinned before You by our indifference;
And for the sin that we have sinned before You by obedience to orders that serve the occupation regime;

And for all of these, we have no right to beg forgiveness, for we did not acknowledge the humanity of Others.

Text of the Yom Kippur Plea for Forgiveness, published by Yesh Gvul as an ad in *Ha'aretz*, 1988.

# The privilege of saying 'No!'

## Adi Ofir

*A young lecturer at the time of his refusal to serve in the occupied territories, Professor Ofir now teaches philosophy at Tel Aviv University. He was a founder member of 'The 21st Year', an anti-occupation movement founded in 1988 in response to the first* intifada. *This is the text of his letter to the then minister of defence Yitzhak Rabin:*

Tomorrow, Monday July 27, I shall report for periodic reserve service with my unit, the artillery battalion of the 252nd Division. Our assignment, according to the call-up notice, is policing actions in the West Bank, including 'contact with the local population'. I wish to notify you hereby that, to my great regret, I cannot agree to take part in fulfilling this assignment, and for the first time after close on twenty years' service as conscript and reservist with a combat unit, I shall be obliged to refuse an order.

My decision to refuse is not a rash one. I have thought it over for a long time and shall carry it out with a heavy heart. I am well aware of the grave import of refusal of orders in any army, in the IDF particularly. I am aware of the harm that such a refusal, should it become a widespread phenomenon, is liable to inflict upon the resilience of the IDF and the integrity of Israeli society. Nevertheless, I shall refuse, because you, honoured Defence Minister, and the government in which you serve, leave me no other choice. Let me expound my reasons.

You advocate the imposition of 'law and order' upon the rebellious populace which, seven months ago, launched into an uprising against Israeli rule. For the first time since the 1967 war, Palestinian resistance to the Israeli occupation has expanded into a systematic campaign embracing most of the Palestinian population. Palestinian enmity towards Zionism has existed for many years; it is profound and menacing, and must be taken into account in any future negotiations. But this is a struggle for freedom which, even if it extends to calls for the destruction of the state of Israel, is in its entirety directed at liberation from Israeli control.

Against popular Palestinian resistance, the IDF under your leadership employs a series of repressive means which will continue to afflict the Jewish national memory. The boundaries between preventative and punitive action have been blurred. Thousands of persons have been penalised without trial, in arbitrary fashion, without the control mechanisms normal to a regulated regime. Again and again, collective punishment actions are applied, inflicting suffering upon the innocent. Again and again, excessive force is applied against rioters, children choke to death on tear gas, babies lose their eyes to rubber bullets. Human rights are trampled upon as daily routine; criminal excesses of various degrees of gravity are continually committed by the authorities and under their aegis, in the twilight zone between law and evil that the occupation regime has created on the far side of the green line, and which has long been spreading to our side too.

The IDF operates in the occupied territories under orders, some of which are flagrantly illegal. Between the militias of the Jewish settlers, maverick soldiers who open fire following illegal rules of engagement, those who detain scores without trial on a daily basis - there has come about a continuum of injustice in entirety under your responsibility and your conductor's baton. Today I am summoned to play an active role in this concert of evil, in which those involved are liable to find themselves implicated in war crimes. I refuse.

From some of your recent utterances it emerges that you too – like certain generals in dictatorial regimes under US patronage – consider observance of human rights and moral limitations on the use of force to be code names for eventual American pressure. For me, as for many other Israelis who have become refuseniks, and for others who have not as yet done so, these are the basic requirements of a regulated democratic society, and the guidelines of the behavioural code of those who live in it. You demand of me today to discard that code, to ignore those basic requirements in the name of that 'national security' for which you bear responsibility; in the name of the rule of law, which you represent in this context; in the name of the resilience of Israeli democracy. In the present political situation, all these grounds for your demand are baseless.

If the Israeli government were to work genuinely for a solution of the Israeli–Palestinian conflict and termination of the occupation; had this government not systematically foiled any peace initiative; had it not ignored signs of moderation and willingness for compromise to be heard here and there on the Palestinian side, it could be claimed that the occupation regime – even when it has lost any semblance of 'enlightenment' – is a necessary evil. If you could come in all honesty on behalf of this government and claim that the acts of oppression in particular, and the occupation regime overall, are a transient interim state of affairs until a settlement is achieved, you could justify my summons to serve with the army of occupation on the grounds of national security. But you, honoured minister, do not come in honesty. The government of which you are a part persists in the policy of its predecessors, acting consistently to perpetuate the occupation rather than to bring about its termination. Like its predecessors, this government too leaves the Palestinians no choice other than to struggle by non-political means to achieve their freedom and realise their right to national existence. Honoured Defence Minister, you have no moral right to call upon me to impose law and order upon them before you open up, in all seriousness, before the Palestinian people, legitimate channels of political struggle. Under present circumstances you do not call me to protect Israel's security; rather, to take part in the continued enslavement of another people.

Accordingly, when you come to justify my summons to service, you cannot honestly do so in the name of democracy. Under the cover of the rubber bullets, tear gas grenades and live ammunition with which you intend to equip me tomorrow, democratic Israel controls the lives of a million and a half Palestinians. Nobody knows better than you that it does so with a heavy hand, with continual denial of basic human rights, and of course, without giving them any share in government. In the years that have elapsed since you were prime minister [Rabin's first term as prime minister was in the years 1974-6] and until you took over the defence portfolio, this situation of running the lives of another people has become permanent, the sole remnant of Israeli democracy being the mask of the parliamentary game within the green line border. Even that mask is fading and fraying before our very eyes, under your full responsibility, with the advanced training you now grant to the IDF in mass detentions and collective punishment, with the Shabak security police behind the scenes, with this all-embracing moral callousness in full view.

Continuation of the occupation is a far greater menace to Israeli democracy than my refusal and that of my colleagues who have already refused, and those who have not yet done so. At this time of stepped-up oppressive measures and the erosion of democratic control mechanisms, our refusal is more than the courage of 'gentle souls' – it's that too, and I'm proud of it ! - but above all, this refusal is a form unparalleled in its responsibility and almost the only way presently possible of playing a role in Israeli society.

Our refusal is an attempt to drive a stake into the slippery slope between democracy and a different regime. It marks a border at a line where, in sequence, there is a blurring of the lines distinguishing a society whose laws express human sublimity, and one whose laws express its degeneration. We are still far from the bottom of the slope, but we are rapidly approaching it. My refusal is justified today, because you, Mr Rabin, and your colleagues in government, no longer provide an adequate guarantee that we will halt before we get there.

On all of these grounds, not even the necessity of protecting the rule of law can justify my summons to reserve duty. For today, you, and the occupation regime in whose running you share, are a far greater threat to the rule of law than masses of refuseniks, if such were to emerge. Mr. Rabin, I – whose refusal stems from the values that are fundamental to any enlightened regime – recognise the authority of the rule of law, and on Monday June 27 1988, I shall present myself for trial, prepared to take the punishment. It is your right, by law if not by dint of justice, to instruct my commanding officers to sentence me to imprisonment for refusing orders. It is your obligation, under law and justice alike, to re-consider where you are leading both the army, where persons like me become refuseniks, and the state, which persons like me serve by refusing to serve in its army.

# Silences that cry out

## Doron Vilner
*A co-founder of Yesh Gvul and long active with its Tel Aviv group, Doron Vilner is currently employed as a social worker. He comes from a well-known family of political activists. His father, Meir, for many years leader of the Israeli Communist Party, was, until his death on 5 June 2003, the last surviving signatory on Israel's 1948 Declaration of Independence.*

'I'm a refusenik,' I explain to those who inquire what I'm doing here in prison. Old-time inmates don't so much as raise an eyebrow in surprise. In Military Prison 6, the presence of refuseniks is a regular feature. Right away, they recall the names of other refuseniks who have been incarcerated here in the past. Part of the prison population are 'returnees', soldiers who leave now and again for a period of regular service with their units, but then go AWOL and return to prison. Other inmates, for whom this is their first ever encounter with a flesh-and-blood refusenik, try to figure out what it is that brings an 'old man' like me to stand on my principles in confrontation with the army over my refusal to serve in the occupied territories. Needless to say, there's no connection between a soldier's opinion about whether or not to restore the occupied territories to 'them' (the Arabs), and his unwillingness to serve in the army at all, or be posted anywhere further from home than a municipal bus ride.

Many of the prison's inmates serve with combat units. Some of them regard prison as a transit point to easier duties, or home (through early release from the army). Others remain proud of their units despite their imprisonment. Their anger and frustration are directed at the particular officer responsible for their imprisonment, rather than at the military apparatus overall. My encounter with these soldiers is the hardest of all.

In inter-personal relations, there are no difficulties. Out of the fraternity of the prisoners, some help me in turning over two of my regulation issue blankets for the 'parade' ('parade' is local parlance for the particularly stupid way of folding blankets; preparations for the 'parade' are among the matters that occupy the minds of those responsible for prison discipline, as well as the time of the convicted conscipts. Each parade entails an examination of the sixteen folds of the blankets).

Convicts approach me for help in writing letters of request or application of various types and categories, addressed to the prison authorities. At the same time, we debate 'return-or-not' in relation to the occupied territories, or 'talk-or-not' with the PLO.

The surprise is the discovery of what it is the occupation does to those who enforce it on the ground. Ostensibly, they're ordinary youngsters like you'd meet anywhere else in the world, who talk about the girl-friend they have or haven't got, or how many days they have left to serve in prison. But over and again, conversations in the tents revert to experiences they've had in fighting the *intifada*. They talk about the Palestinian they beat to a pulp; about the child they caught after a chase, and how his mother came along and made such a fuss trying to get him released; about the Ratz (Liberal) party member who handed over the Arab he'd caught to the Border Guards, begging them not to beat 'his' Arab, and how they just waited for him to clear off before giving the prisoner a thrashing. Whenever I enter the tent, the talk ceases or they change the subject to more general matters.

Those silences cry out. I have often heard stories of such silences. I heard about them in another land [Germany] when an entire generation kept silent, never telling their children about an entire period of their lives. And here in prison, detached from my usual circle of acquaintances, I meet those who do the daily work of the occupation. An entire generation for whom authorised establishment violence is part of their daily round.

In corners, when there aren't many listeners around and you can talk discreetly, someone finds a moment to slip up to me and say he didn't behave that way, that he was different. And anyway, they too, the Arabs, are human beings.

# Benighted fanaticism

### Nitzan Levy

As a citizen committed to the state of Israel, I refuse postings to service in the occupied territories, to take part in the repression of the civil uprising of the population that's been living under the yoke of Israeli occupation – however 'enlightened' it may be – for over 20 years and now wishing to take its fate into its own hands.

As a soldier, I am no longer willing to stand facing these people, whether masked or unmasked, to continue to shed their blood on behalf of vague values such as: restoring calm, there's no alternative, we have to teach 'em a lesson or re-educate them. All this in support of the argument that this is a job that has to be done until the politicians can make up their minds on the political objective.

I am convinced that relying exclusively on military force in these circumstances generates inevitable erosion in my mentality as a soldier, undermining values such as: 'fighting spirit', 'combat morals', and even 'Israeli security'. Continuation of this destructive trend demolishes the delicate fibre of Israeli society, bringing to the surface more and more manifestations of racism, extreme nationalism and benighted fanaticism, all resting upon 'plastic' and 'rubber' bullets and live ammunition.

In these difficult circumstances, there is no refuge for anyone in Israel wishing to be humane, only the narrow and humiliating tunnel offered by military prison. Will we rest content with that?

# A typical 'NO' poem

## Nathan Zach

*Nathan Zach is an illustrious Israeli poet and a consistent supporter of Yesh Gvul and the refusal movement.*

Because we may not have the time to move mountains
And it may be we didn't come here to move mountains
But we have a little time to compose poems
About the great privilege of being here below
About the great privilege of saying 'No'.

# A policy that demeans my country

## Shaul Schwartz

*Although open heart surgery undergone in his youth made him eligible for exemption, Shaul Schwartz insisted on completing his compulsory 3-year service. His release certificate extolled him as 'an excellent soldier, exhibiting exceptional motivation and intellectual initiative'. A cellist with the Rehovot Orchestra, a music teacher and a sergeant in the airforce reserve, Schwartz received 3 consecutive jail sentences for refusing to serve as guard at the Keziot detention camp where thousands of Palestinians were being held without trial.*

Like many others in this land, I sense discomfort over the existence of these camps where thousands are held without trial, while thousands more are sentenced under military law arising out of the policy of occupation justified by the claim that 'there's no alternative'. But no genuine step has been taken to change the situation. This policy gives the two peoples thousands of reasons to hate each other, to throw stones and Molotov cocktails, to stab and shoot and kill.

I am no longer willing to serve a policy that prejudices the basic rights of every human being. Nor to lend a hand to a policy that demeans my country. Before every act of refusal, I applied for alternative duty that would not run counter to my conscience. That privilege was not granted me. I am glad I have the strength to fight for it.

# The refusenik answers the writer*
## Mario Weinstein in correspondence with Yizhar Smilansky

*Born in Argentina, Mario Weinstein emigrated to Israel in 1965, where he worked as a journalist, editor of the Spanish language journal* **Aurora**, *and translator. Weinstein is married with two children.*

*Yizhar Smilansky is a well-known Israeli writer and novelist of doveish views, which are reflected in his stories of the 1948 Arab-Israeli war. Notable among them are 'Hirbet Hizat' and 'The Prisoner', both of which depict IDF soldiers who witness, but do not speak out against, human rights abuses committed by their comrades in arms. Like many mainline peaceniks, Smilansky is opposed to refusal of service in the occupied territories, though he couches his criticism in moderate terms. The following exchange of letters between Smilansky and his friend, refusenik Mario Weinstein, began while the latter was in jail.*

Dear Mario,
So you went to prison rather than do your reserve duty in the occupied territories? I understand why you did it, and ask myself whether I wouldn't do the same, rather than play the role of occupier.

Anyone who isn't torn between the call to obey his duties as soldier in the army of occupation, and the call to obey the duty of an honest man, is

* Published in the daily *Davar*, February 1990.

either a man who never asks questions, or he's inhumane, caring above all for himself and his tribe.

But while military prison may offer a hygienic solution for the problem of the individual soldier, it provides no answer for the true dilemma: how to seal up the national sewage pit.

For it is out of the question not to serve in the IDF, even as it presently is. It's out of the question to leave the army 'cleansed' of those who detest the occupation, it's out of the question to leave the army to 'them'. The main point is, the army isn't to blame for the occupation, it's the politicians who send it there – they and they alone are the objective of a personal and public struggle, political and historical.

The country is now run by a leadership that is united and patient in enforcing the occupation, indifferent to death, havoc and destruction, in some dull expectation of a Judgement Day when the Prophet Elijah will bring the capitulation of the Arabs, that will be termed 'peace'.

We could have ended this superfluous and degrading occupation long ago, and with far greater gains, were this leadership wiser, braver, more honest, and above all, interested in peace; but it isn't wise, nor brave, nor honest, and above all, it isn't interested in anything but forcing the other side to surrender.

It's this political leadership that should be fought. If not during the one month of reserve duty, then throughout the other eleven months of the year when the citizen-soldier is free to attack, to raise hell, to recruit others for the great national refusal.

Incarceration in prison is difficult, offensive and depressing – while also purifying and protesting and setting an example; but that isn't the way to the great national refusal. It's not in prison that the great decisions will be reached, but outside, in the street, out loud and with all your strength. These brave soldiers who opted to be honest men in prison so as not to be soldiers of the occupation – why don't they set out, with all their moral vigour, to raise their voices outside, to call for the great national refusal and spread the flame into the mind of every Jew?

You should serve in the IDF. You shouldn't go to prison. The main thing isn't personal purity, it's breaking the blockage of our national sewage.

•••

Dear Yizhar,

I read your letter over and over again, after you were good enough to send it to me here in prison prior to its publication. Ostensibly, it seems to indicate that we share the same ideas, and agree on the desirable solution, but disagree on the means. In military terms, our differences are tactical rather than strategic.

But our unique circumstances – which have taken us to the outer boundaries of sanity, to the line between good and evil, between permissible and forbidden, between the human and the bestial – have led me to the conclusion that there is no separating the way from the means, between course and objective. We are walking a tightrope over a chasm, and the slightest slip could lead to disaster. And so, the means are the objective, the way – the destination.

Let me put it differently. If it's true that you should think ahead of where you're going, the converse also holds true, and the final calamity is brought on by absence of prior reflection. If the policy in force today is leading (or liable to lead) to a situation where a uniformed soldier aims (without firing) at a ten-year-old child, this entire policy is unworthy from the outset, and it must be changed, or altered, at all events rejected in disgust.

I reject the debate over the issue of who is in the right, we or the Palestinians. It's irrelevant to the subject under discussion. There are absolute situations, situations which under no circumstances can be made relative. An armed soldier facing a child is such an absolute situation, and I don't care what led to that situation, who is in the right or what the conflict is about.

Anyone willing nowadays to serve in the occupied territories in the role of occupier is liable to find himself in such a situation, even against his will. Whosoever agrees to go there thus agrees from the outset, whether consciously or not, to get into that situation. And after all, there are things that a Jew is forbidden to do, so you told me once.

You write that 'military prison may offer a hygienic solution for the problem of the individual soldier' and I agree with every word. But your words imply a measure of disdain for this solution because it doesn't enfold 'the solution to the real dilemma', and you of course refer to the national dilemma.

Exceptional persons speak of the nation. Among ordinary mortals and soldiers from the ranks, each takes care of his own conscience. It's small, it's modest, but that's what we've got. And in the name of the great, noble and sublime – but somewhat abstract - concept of 'nation', we shall have to commit mass murder of small, private and selfish consciences: for they are the only ones that actually exist.

I'm out of prison now. The day of my release, when I got home, I went over to the shelf and hauled out your book, re-reading the final lines of *The Prisoner*. Each word, dear Yizhar, sank in like water to a thirsty soul, restoring my spirits and reinforcing my convictions. I prefer to act in accordance with what is written there, rather than what you recommended in your letter.

Yours respectfully,
Mario

## On the festival of freedom I waive my freedom Or: What shall I tell my daughter?

### Dubi Hayun

*At the time of his refusal, Dubi Hayun was a member of Kibbutz Ramat Rachel on the southern outskirts of Jerusalem. He was the editor of the kibbutz periodical* Shdemot. *Just ahead of the Jewish religious festival of Passover 1990, Hayun refused to serve in the occupied territories, preferring to spend the traditional festival of freedom behind bars.*

There are moments when a person has to pay the price of his words.

I read in the press about 'good souls' who return from reserve service in the occupied territories and deplore what is going on there, but next time they get their call-up papers they send back the okay and return to duty. 'They shoot and cry.'

In August 1988, eight months after the onset of the *intifada*, I served in the Jabaliya Palestinian refugee camp in the Gaza Strip. Then too, I was in two minds whether or not to refuse. What tilted the balance was the thought that perhaps my presence there could prevent outrages. After a couple of days, I realised my mistake. You can't do anything against the horrors going on there.

After a week and a half, I got the chance of a release; I grabbed it and ran for my life. Some days later came the murder by beating of Palestinian Hanni al Hashmi at the IDF Jabaliya military strongpoint. Sadly, I was not surprised. During the few days I served there, I saw Palestinian prisoners beaten and humiliated, ten-year-olds beaten and intimidated and so on and so forth. Once the club is raised, it flails indiscriminately, and fatal beatings are the outcome.

What I saw with my own eyes is witnessed by thousands of soldiers serving in the occupied territories, right-wingers and left-wingers who stand together and progressively lose their humanity, their moral freedom, as they rob another people of its physical freedom....

When my daughter asks me about it, I'll tell her one mustn't be silent; one must cry out, even at the price of time in jail. Some will ask me whether I am preaching evasion of duty or violation of the law. My reply is a brief quote from Martin Luther King Junior's *Letter from a Birmingham Jail* (1964):

> *I don't preach evasion or violation of the law. That would lead to anarchy. A man who violates unjust laws must do so openly, out of love and a willingness to accept the penalty. The individual who breaks the law that his conscience tells him is an unjust law, and who willingly accepts the penalty of imprisonment so to awaken the communal conscience to the injustice, truly expresses the highest measure of respect for the law.*

And I'm willing to pay the price, lovingly. This festival of freedom – I waive my freedom so as to cry out against the theft of the physical freedom of an entire people, and against the application of laws that are unjust, and against the deprivation of our moral freedom.

At the festival of freedom, I waive my own freedom.

# No to 'always at command'*

## Danny Zamir

*A member of Kibbutz Ayelet Hashahar and an officer in the reserves, Danny Zamir was sentenced on 22 April 1990 to 28 days for refusal to serve in Nablus. Zamir now heads the kibbutz movement's preparatory seminar for youngsters ahead of their induction into the army.*

'Two things,' wrote the German philosopher Kant, 'fill the human spirit with wonder and awe: the star-strewn skies above and the moral sense within.'

What wonderful, noble sentiments! But they are meaningless in the central point of our discussion: what is the link and the commitment

---

* 'Always at Command' was the battle hymn of the Jewish elite militia Palmach, which was initially illegal under the British mandate and later became the shock troops of the nascent Israeli army in the 1948 fighting.

between my daily preoccupations and that inner moral sense, and what, if anything is the yardstick for judging my actions, particularly when they clash with immoral actions, such as misguided laws of the land?

Some 150 years after Kant, in a steamy young coastal city on the eastern Mediterranean, a man no longer young, nor a naive 'noble dove' [the term adversaries use to deprecate 'peaceniks'] proclaimed the following:

> *The state of Israel … shall rest upon foundations of freedom, justice and peace, in the light of the vision of the prophets of Israel; the state shall maintain complete social and political equal rights for all its citizens, irrespective of religion, race or gender; it shall ensure freedom of religion, conscience, education and culture; protect the Holy Places of all religions and be faithful to the Charter of the United Nations.* *

Today, the spring of 1990, almost 42 years later, I feel like one of the residents of Pompei, who see the volcano seethe under their feet, sending up clouds of steam, about to explode at any moment and threatening to inundate them in great waves of lava and a thick layer of ash.

With stupid resolve and the smugness of the all-knowing, primitive preachers and unbridled nationalists are leading and misleading us to calamity, while Pompei is preoccupied with watching boxing matches, and with banquets in advance of the disaster. 'Stupid, where do you see any volcano?', ask the Pompeians, directing their gaze westwards towards the sea.

I see a volcano in a land where one third of the inhabitants are banned, by dint of their national and ethnic origins and geographical location, from voting as equals, where they do not have basic civic rights and where thousands are detained under administrative decree (i.e. without trial and for an unlimited period) under a military justice system that is farcical.

A land, a third of whose inhabitants have been subjected to extended military occupation for over 20 years – which means restriction of rights and a different code of law for the Jewish and Arab residents of the selfsame land – is not a democratic country. As such, it consciously denies its basic and substantive commitments (to itself and its inhabitants) as proclaimed and declared by its first prime minister – that declaration which serves to this day as the basis of its fragile democracy.

Accordingly, collaboration with a regime or government that forces or orders me to be part of an anti-democratic apparatus which leads to self-

---

* From the Charter of Independence, proclaimed by David Ben Gurion, Israel's first prime minister, 14 May 1948.

destruction, disintegration and national decay, along with utter denial of its own foundations, is illegitimate, unjust and immoral. And it will remain so as long as the state does not take one of the only two feasible actions: annexation of all or most of the territories conquered in 1967 and granting of full civic rights to those residing there; or withdrawal from densely populated areas and a settlement that will release us of responsibility for the residents of those areas, who will choose for themselves whatever regime they desire (of course, with security arrangements included).

Collaboration with the regime, the government, which for 22 years has made no significant step in that direction, is in my view entirely unacceptable. Even if it is only a minority that is aware thereof, and even if only an even smaller minority is willing to pay the price.

Next Sunday I shall be tried for something of which I am innocent, when the real charge on which I am to be judged as grounds for refusal is the fact that I am a true Zionist democrat aspiring to survive.

The majority will continue to hum 'Always at Command' and history will judge – as ever, too late – as it has judged other evil and stupid regimes.

*After his release from 28 days' detention, Danny Zamir gave the following speech at a kibbutz convention:*

I'm a nice kibbutz boy. My CV shows a year of voluntary social service prior to my three years in the army, and five years with the paratroops as company commander. After the army I returned to my kibbutz. I didn't have any wild ideas in my head, I didn't even take the customary trip abroad [traditional among many Israelis on conclusion of their military service]. And yet, for being true to the values on which I'd been brought up, I was sent to prison and suspended from my post as company commander. It was not fortuitous that the criticism levelled against me in the kibbutz came from the younger generation who had grown up on myth. As they saw it, any challenge to the army as an institution undermines the whole structure.

I refused to serve in the occupied territories because opposition to the occupation has to be systematic and overall. When we serve in the territories, all of us – the battalion commander, the company commander and the ordinary soldier – are pawns in somebody's game. There's no distinction between them.

Out of 25,000 Palestinians indicted and put on trial, seven were found not guilty, or it may have been eleven – what's the odds? Anyone who serves there serves that apparatus. 'Legality', 'law', 'justice' – all these may exist for Jewish citizens of Israel. The terms are meaningless in the occupied territories.

Youngsters brought up in the kibbutz are not unique in the moral sense; the three officers indicted for deliberately breaking the arms and legs of the Palestinian villagers of Huwara were kibbutz youngsters, and I know they were brought up on the identical values. It's the occupation that obliges you to commit the worst of offences, makes no difference who you are.

The refusal movement will not destroy the army nor undermine democracy. It is a legitimate democratic act to refuse when you're willing to pay the price. If the country is genuinely democratic, it should be attentive to the feelings of its citizens. Refusal on a massive scale will oblige the government to launch into a dialogue with the Palestinians.

## Born on the Fourth of July

*The American movie* Born on the Fourth of July, *with Tom Cruise, tells the story of American GIs wounded in Vietnam who grasped they had been duped and organized vigorous protests against the war. The film, shown during the first intifada, enjoyed great success in Israel. Seizing on the movie's anti-war message – and its stress on resistance by soldiers – Yesh Gvul members handed out the following leaflet to movie-goers leaving the cinemas:*

How was the movie? Gripping? Moving? Food for thought? 'He was born on the 4th of July'. He went to war young, goodlooking, strong – and returned in a wheelchair, a broken man; he went full of hope and faith – and returned in despair; he went full of idealism – and found that it was all a lie, that he had been swindled; he went to fight for his country – and found himself killing babies and innocent people ...

Does it sound familiar? He was born on the 4th of July – when were you born? When will we all wake up?

An end to murder and repression in the occupied territories!

Bring the soldiers home!

# 'You don't have to do anything wicked'

## Daniel Padnes

*Daniel Padnes is active in Beit Gefen, the Jewish-Arab culture centre in Haifa. He was sentenced to 28 days for refusal on 1 November 1990.*

As a new immigrant to Israel, I did not enlist in the IDF when I was younger. In fact, the army waited until I had completed my bachelor's degree before calling me to serve. I made no objections. By this, I thought, I will fulfil my civic duties. Apart from that, service would finally provide me with a response to my right-wing friends who took great pleasure during our political arguments in saying: 'What do you know about it all? You haven't even served in the army!'

The location of the basic training camp on the West Camp was not to my liking. But what could I do, there was no similar base within the 'green line' [pre-1967 Israel]. So I compromised.

Then came the Saturday when it was decided to send us to the al-Para'a refugee camp, to seek out terrorists who had infiltrated from Jordan. Okay, you have to defend your country. When I got there, they had already hauled out all the men from the camp, concentrating them in a field encompassed by a fence. I told my section commander I was afraid I would have to disobey orders. 'Nonsense!', he said, 'You don't have to do anything wicked, just patrol the camp.' He gave me a gentle push, helped me over the wall of the school, and suddenly I was inside the refugee camp, and again, I compromised.

I completed four months of basic training, and two months later, Israel invaded Lebanon. I resolved to make no further compromises. I joined Yesh Gvul and anxiously awaited my call-up papers. But they didn't arrive. Somehow or other, my name was omitted. Each time I got my call-up, it was for service inside Israel, not in Lebanon. A matter of chance.

Whenever some left-wing group held an event or lecture about service in the occupied territories, I was there. Should one serve, or carry out duties in an 'enlightened' manner? Where should I draw the line? I underwent considerable soul-searching. With the outbreak of the *intifada* in December 1987, I knew beyond doubt that my personal limit was the 'green line'. I also knew it was only a matter of time.

The next October, just as I was planning a trip out of the country, I got a call-up for November. To receive permission to leave the country, I signed an undertaking to return in time for my reserve duty. I went off on my trip, and just as I was about to return, I got an urgent call from home: 'We've heard you're to be assigned to service in Gaza. Are you sure you want to return ?' Of course I wanted to return. Was I some kind of criminal scared to return home ? I returned and set off to the military base specified.

The sign read: 'Training centre'. I got there in time for a training session. Various types of tear gas, 'plastic' bullets, rubber-coated bullets, small bombs that hurl fragments in all directions. The guys sat there and listened, looking at one another in confusion, then they went to bed.

'Don't worry,' said my section officer, 'We know about your problem. We'll find you an assignment entailing no direct contact with the population.'

'What's that about?' I demanded, 'I'll stay in camp and prepare rations for the others, to keep up their stamina so they can chase after the Palestinian kids? Thanks, but no thanks.'

'So what d'you want me to do with you ?'

'Find me a different assignment, inside the green line.'

'Sorry, there aren't any this time.'

'Sorry sir,' I replied, 'this time, I refuse.'

I'd reached my decision. But that wasn't the end of it. I didn't expect my own soul-searching to be passed on now to my officer. We were in the field, in a camp without a telephone link to brigade HQ. 'There's no point you coming with us to Gaza,' the officer said. 'Go on home and wait there till you hear from the company commander.' Home? As simple as that? Unbelievable.

On my way, I was approached by my best friend in the unit, a social worker by profession. 'Think it over, Daniel,' he said. I explained that I had reached my decision years ago, and it was only on technical grounds that it had never been put into effect. He tried to change my mind, arguing that I didn't really want to go to jail, it was just that I felt obliged towards my leftist friends. 'What about your friends in the company?' he demanded. 'Don't they bear some consideration?'

I thought it over there and then. It was true. I was refusing for my friends on the left; I was refusing for every Palestinian man or woman who had ever stood up for a political solution to the conflict with Israel, and for co-existence; and for every peace-loving man or woman anywhere in the world, those who believe in non-violence as a way towards change. But above all, perhaps, for my own sake: so as not to render ludicrous ten years of endeavour for peace and co-existence.

I refused, and was sentenced to a month in jail. I was the only refusenik in jail at the time. But there was one question that bothered me: 'What will you do if you are called again and again? Will you refuse each time? Will you become a permanent resident at Military Prison No. 6?' It was a painful question, and a painful prospect.

# Decent people don't shoot children

## Itamar Pitovsky

*Itamar Pitovsky is professor of philosophy at the Hebrew University, Jerusalem. He was jailed for refusal in 1992.*

'Be a good soldier,' they tell you when you're a kid. 'And also, a thinking person.' 'Draw a distinction between good and evil.' As long as it's a matter of mood or states of consciousness – what the philosophers call 'intentional situations' – it's okay. Furthermore, your soul-searching makes you a better soldier. But the moment these states of consciousness transfer into the behavioural level, the moment your intentions hit upon the appropriate action, then the entire dialectic card castle collapses: a recalcitrant soldier – a refusenik – has no place in Israeli society.

The state of mind known as 'shooting-and-crying' now faces its testing moment. It is not the first test, but certainly it is the most severe. It is not fortuitous that anthologies like *Soldiers' Discourse* [a series of soul-searching discussions, rather tearful monologues and breast-beating by IDF soldiers published shortly after the 1967 war and long a favourite with Israeli liberals] don't get composed nowadays. What could they write ? Imagine the picture of a soldier brandishing his club in a refugee camp in Gaza, while simulta-neously his mind is filled with *Soldiers' Discourse*-like reflections ('Maybe this man is a farmer? Maybe a worker? The mere fact that such thoughts come to life …' and so on and so forth.) Now really! There's a limit to absurdity.

It is against that absurdity I protest and refuse to take part therein, for a simple reason: Decent people don't shoot children. All other matters – democracy, politics, what people will say – are secondary and marginal in relation to that fundamental awareness. Even if it is proven to me beyond any shadow of a doubt that my decision to refuse service in the occupied territories entails 'political harm' – and I don't think it does – even then, I will persist in my refusal. There are matters in relation to which the fact that man is a political creature becomes irrelevant. The killing of children is such a matter.

# I owe my children at least one refusal

## Dan Sagir

*Formerly a journalist with the daily* Ha'aretz, *Dan Sagir now runs a translation agency in Jerusalem.*

In the late 1980s, my job as military correspondent for the daily *Ha'aretz* required me to interview numerous IDF soldiers and officers about their motivation for duty in the occupied territories. Those were the peak years of the [first] *intifada,* and the military unit charged with checking morale produced lots of reassuring studies. In hindsight, they were right. Refusal to serve in the occupied territories was a marginal manifestation; most soldiers, conscripts or reservists, set off for the occupied territories to do whatever was demanded of them, without any particular success in suppressing the Palestinian uprising.

Like thousands of other high school graduates conscripted after the 1973 Yom Kippur war, I too joined up and served with the armoured corps just recovering from its mauling in the recently ended fighting. It was natural for me to head for the officers' course; my motivation was high. When the *intifada* erupted in 1987, it was self-evident to me that I would serve, for refusal was a matter for the radical left. But in hindsight, a couple of biographical facts played their part.

Two years earlier, I had reported from South Africa on the black riots against the *apartheid* regime. The Palestinian uprising fascinated me. Young persons and children – not starched politicians – became the leaders, setting the tone and creating a new political situation. I wanted to serve in the occupied territories so as to expand my view of events. Another biographical detail was my journalistic calling. I asked the editor for a transfer at the first available opportunity from my economic brief to coverage of military matters, so as to be 'involved'.

Journalistic involvement in political or social conflict is among the few really important privileges I found in this profession. You get the illusion that you have some slight influence in the direction you believe in. If you write, I thought, you have no call to do anything else, such as going to jail for refusal to serve in the occupied territories.

The *intifada* came to an end and Yitzhak Rabin, who had been defence minister during the uprising, led a courageous *démarche* towards reconciliation with the Palestinians. Rabin and Shimon Peres thereby joined other brave individuals we have witnessed this past decade: de Klerk and Mandela in South Africa, Gorbachev in the Soviet Union, and the rest is history. At the most crucial moment of completion of the interim agreements with the Palestinians, the government was replaced.

I remained optimistic. I believed the peace process was irreversible and would overcome its enemies in the government. In view of recent events, that optimism has bled to death, along with soldiers and officers and other victims from both sides at various locations in the occupied territories.

Officers like me don't get summoned to morale-boosting conventions. There's no need. We come along, do our duty, and then go home quietly. But this week something inside me broke. As a father of three, I had hoped to give them a better future. That hope is rapidly evaporating. If my children are required, a few years from now, to go to Gaza, to combat *intifada* Number Three, Four or Five, I owe them at least one refusal to serve in the occupied territories. Perhaps if we – the gray backbone of the reserve units – lose no time in registering our objections, the peace process will be put back on course.

I have a few months up to my next term of service in the occupied territories. As matters stand, they can get a cot ready for me at Military Prison No. 4. I want to look my children in the eyes and tell them I did everything I could, not merely as a journalist, to give them a better country.

# The Philosophy of Selective Refusal

**Peretz Kidron**

'Selective refusal' is arguably the Israeli peace movement's most original contribution to the 'arsenal' of anti-militarist protest, with its application of the code of civil disobedience, as forged by Gandhi and Martin Luther King, to that least likely of settings, the army.

Unlike revolution, which challenges the overall political *status quo* in all its aspects, civil disobedience focuses on a specific injustice or abuse, homing in on a law or regulation that embodies its essence and picking out that law or regulation for systematic and overt defiance (in the US South, the target was public transport, which exemplified the most rampant and glaring form of racial discrimination; Gandhi chose to flout the British colonial authorities' ban on 'unauthorised' production of salt). Accordingly, the refusal movement – as a prominent element of Israel's domestic opposition – has focussed on the IDF and its key role in enforcing the occupation of Palestinian territories or the invasion of Lebanon. In choosing to challenge the law requiring soldiers to serve where and as ordered, IDF refuseniks do not engage in all-out mutiny: rather, with a *chutzpeh* unheard of in other armies, they place themselves on a par with the generals and politicians in judging overall policy, and arrogate to themselves the prerogative of choosing, by their own lights, which orders to obey or disobey.

My first introduction to selective refusal was in Paris on 14 July 1951, as I watched the Communist Party's Bastille Day procession. It was a mighty demonstration, tens of thousands of marchers taking over the city centre. A principle theme of the march was opposition to the colonial war France was then conducting in Indo-China (present-day Vietnam, Laos and Cambodia). The slogan, echoing and re-echoing, was a *Paix à Vietnam, libérez Henri Martin!* (Peace in Vietnam, free Henri Martin!)

Who was Henri Martin? I learned that the young man had willingly enlisted for his term of service with the French navy, but when ordered to

Vietnam, had refused to take part in the campaign of represson, and was jailed. His act of defiance evoked considerable public sympathy, but failed to prompt a broad refusal movement in the French armed forces. I salute Martin as 'my' first selective refusenik.

## What is selective refusal?

Selective refusal was shaped by the complex military-political parameters created by the 1967 war. In its wake, a generation of soldiers brought up on the myth of the Israel Defense Forces discovered overnight that the broadly legitimate defensive duties they had discharged hitherto were now replaced by the task of policing a subject Palestinian civilian population. That abrupt change came as a major shock to a segment of IDF reservists. The small but vocal protest movement already campaigning against the occupation counted in its ranks numerous men of military age routinely called to annual reserve service, frequently in the occupied territories. Thus, after denouncing the occupation for eleven months in the year, many a left-winger found himself in the perplexing predicament of being drafted to spend the twelfth month enforcing that selfsame occupation!

The dilemma was intolerable. Moral reflex rebelled against service with an army of occupation. But regional realities still posed threats: at least in theory, external aggression might yet restore the IDF to its professed defensive role. Accordingly, very few could bring themselves to outright rejection of all forms of army service. Inevitably, a line was drawn between 'legitimate' duties arising from the IDF's potential or actual defensive role, and 'unacceptable' assignments in the occupied territories. (By contrast, South Africa's anti-conscription campaigners of the *apartheid* era rejected all military service, not on pacifist grounds but in response to political realities: in the absence of any external threat, the South African army was entirely engaged in racist repression, leaving no distinction between more or less acceptable duties.)

In December 1972, when IDF reservists Yossi Kotten and Yitzhak Laor stunned the Israeli public by overt defiance of orders to serve in the occupied territories, they hastened to declare their willingness to undertake other, more legitimate duties. 'Selective refusal' was born.

## Moral impact of refuseniks

This form of protest turned out most telling. While those who refuse outright to enlist leave themselves open to charges of shirking or evasion of 'national defence', the refuseniks were seasoned soldiers; in time, their ranks extended to include many who had hitherto rendered distinguished service in frontline combat units. During the Lebanon war, and subsequently, when Yesh Gvul published its anti-war and anti-occupation petitions, they gained additional moral and political weight with the public when the signatories included captains and majors who had won their insignia of rank by years of dedicated service.

In addition to their broader political impact, refuseniks exercise a direct moral effect on the army units to which they belong. The refusal of a few soldiers, or even just one single individual, has an electrifying effect on their comrades-in-arms, obliging them to search their own souls and query the legitimacy of the campaign in which they are engaged.

The moral impact is heightened by a further aspect of selective refusal: defiance of orders is up-front, with no attempt at disguise, thus deliberately courting disciplinary action by the military hierarchy. There are countless ways of evading reserve duty, and thousands of Israelis resort to 'gray refusal' by faking medical disorders, or taking a carefully timed trip abroad ahead of their call-up. But refuseniks reject the personal convenience of such ruses, choosing instead, as a matter of principle, to declare their refusal outright.

By accepting punishment for their defiance of the legal authority of their superiors, refuseniks highlight the depth of their convictions. In glaring contrast to the 'shoot-and-cry' syndrome of those who protested the Lebanon campaign or the occupation of the Palestinian territories but nevertheless meekly reported for duty there whenever summoned, refuseniks demonstrate that their opposition is not merely verbal. Their willingness to pay the price of their moral and political convictions has granted the refuseniks a broad political impact out of all proportion to their actual numbers.

### Conscripts v. career soldiers

It is a matter of record that in the entire annals of Israel's refusenik movement, there has never been a single instance of refusal by a career soldier. It is hardly a matter for surprise. An individual who joins the army of his own free will is generally one disposed to fit into its norms, and obey orders.

But Yesh Gvul records contain a number of letters from retired career officers in the US army who confess to having obeyed orders they now feel in hindsight they 'should have refused'. The numerous cases of rebelliousness in the US army in Vietnam, which contributed significantly to the decision of US military and political leaders to pull out of Vietnam, were mainly the acts of draftees. The US army in Vietnam was mainly draftees, and when they realised the senselessness and futility of that campaign, many units showed a marked disinclination to fight.

Shortly after the end of the Vietnam campaign, in the 1970s, the draft was effectively abolished, and the US army became a volunteer force of career soldiers. This change may explain why American forces now obediently carry out any mission handed down by their political masters, with scarcely a sign of dissent or protest.

In view of the current trend in many countries to move towards a career army, it is important to note this distinction between a conscript army and a force of volunteers, who are in fact mercenaries willing to obey without question. Liberals and left-wingers press for an alternative to conscription – service in social institutions, after the German model – in the well-meaning but erroneous conviction that the opportunity to opt out of compulsory military duty is an effective means of diminishing militarist traditions that have brutalised successive generations. This hope is unfounded, for the simple reason that as long as an army continues to exist, basing it upon those youngsters who volunteer to join acts as a sieve that screens out precisely those elements most likely to reject unworthy duties. To put it bluntly: 'alternative civilian service' channels those youngsters with a social con-science and a developed political awareness into work in hospitals and homes for the elderly, and creates the danger that the armed forces will become the exclusive domain of gungho militarists, skinheads and neo-Nazis!

Conversely, an army based upon conscription creates scope for efforts to educate its soldiers and teach them their legal, moral and political responsibility for the tasks they discharge. As 'citizens in uniform', they can and should be taught that not every task or duty to which they are directed is necessarily the proper role of an army. Quite apart from the more glaring examples of military units that have committed war crimes and human rights abuses, there have been numerous instances of a government employing its armed forces to break domestic strikes by drafting in the army to replace the striking workers. It is ironical that many of the soldiers seconded to be 'uniformed scabs' are brothers or sons of the strikers. Surely such a situation should require a soldier to ask himself whether his military duties – nominally in the cause of 'national security' – include intervention in domestic labour disputes, against the interests of his own friends and relatives.

In the more frequent cases where an army is despatched to carry out aggressive operations against another country, or engage in repression of a civilian population, it is vital that efforts be made to enlighten the soldiers about the impropriety of the orders they receive. The educational work carried out by Yesh Gvul has focussed largely on this aspect, reminding IDF soldiers that they bear personal responsibility for the orders they obey.

## The limits to obedience

Similar efforts should be made in regard to any army. In view of atrocities committed in the past, many armies now go through the motions of informing inductees about international humanitarian law. But this is hardly a task to be entrusted to the very generals who are most likely to order their soldiers to violate these norms. The matter takes on redoubled urgency in view of the enormous lethal and destructive capacity of a modern army.

In every country, alongside every army, it is therefore vital to create organisations independent of government or military control, to undertake the task of educating soldiers, teaching them that compliance with the orders of their superiors is proper and correct under normal circumstances, but also teaching them that obedience must have its limits, which are defined and dictated by the moral conscience and social awareness of each individual.

'Yesh Gvul' is the Hebrew term for 'There's a limit!', implying that there is a limit to obedience. That concept deserves to be translated into every language, for the benefit of every army the world around.

# The Story of Yuval and Imad

Yuval Lotem was 40 in 1997, living in Kfar Shmaryahu just outside Tel Aviv. Unmarried, with a daughter of five, he worked in movie production and script-writing, after originally training as a mechanical engineer.

Like others, Yuval was an army reservist. His military career hitherto had seen its ups and downs. During his regular service, he served with an elite reconnaissance unit before being admitted to the airforce's highly prestigious pilot-training programme, which he however left before completing. He went on to an officers' training course and completed his service as lieutenant with the paratroopers.

After his discharge, he set off, like many young Israelis, to tour the world, spending over two years in Africa. It was a time for reflection about his direction in life. Although he had no direct family connections with the Holocaust, it was a subject that occupied his mind. Whenever he met young Germans, he would question them about what it was that had motivated the genocide. One answer he got left him particularly horrified: 'Everybody did it'. For Yuval, that terse observation was a striking lesson in the dangers of conformism, although he is careful to draw no comparison between the Holocaust and conditions in the occupied territories.

Yuval returned to Israel in the summer of 1982, shortly after the invasion of Lebanon. When called up for reserve service in Lebanon, he refused to go. Henceforth, whenever called to serve in Lebanon or the occupied Palestinian territories, he refused. On the whole, his superiors treated him leniently, his military record standing him in good stead, and his 'insubordination' went unpunished. But on one occasion, in 1993, he refused a posting to the Gaza Strip. 'I couldn't see myself coming and going, in officer's uniform with gun in hand, in the homes of Gaza people.' On this occasion, his luck did not hold: a commanding officer new to the unit refused to let him off and Yuval spent 28 days in military prison.

When the renewed call-up came in 1997, ostensibly 'to guard settle-ments', Yuval decided to adopt a less confrontational course, and did not declare outright that he would refuse to serve in the occupied territories. On reporting for duty, he was sent initially to a post inside pre-1967 Israel, whereupon he put his superiors on notice that, whatever the circumstances, he would not cross the green line. As the unit prepared to take up its positions, a young woman officer announced that two officers were needed 'for another assignment', and Yuval was chosen. When he inquired where he was being sent, he was told only that it would be 'inside the green line'. Requesting more specific information, he was told: 'Megiddo prison'.

Megiddo (the Biblical 'Armageddon') is indeed located inside pre-1967 Israel. But Yuval knew that the prison housed hundreds of Palestinian detainees, many of them 'administratives' incarcerated without the semblance of due judicial process. This was not an assignment he intended to take on. Foreseeing what might lie ahead, Yuval made a detour to his home to pick up a stock of books. Then he went on to Megiddo ('If you don't report, you're a deserter or AWOL, and that's not my game'). Arriving at the prison, Yuval reported to the battalion commander, saying, 'Hello, there's just one small problem, I won't do my reserve duty at Megiddo prison'. After a brief silence the officer said, 'Let's talk about it.' Seeming to take Yuval's declaration as youthful folly, he sent him home to think it over in the hope he'd change his mind. A few hours later the commander called and said: 'Come tomorrow with all your gear, you're on Saturday duty'. Yuval replied he wouldn't do duty at Megiddo, but the officer pulled a trick (associated in Israeli folklore with Likud politician Benyamin Netanyahu), saying there was static on the line and he couldn't hear. But he added he would meet Yuval halfway: he would just be in the command post and do jeep patrols around the camp, without contact with the prisoners.

The next day Yuval reported at the prison, finding another officer and telling him roundly that holding administrative detainees without trial was a criminal act and he didn't intend to become an accomplice to a crime.

Sunday 26 June, the battalion commander turned up and called him in for a talk, stressing he was giving him a last chance. Yuval said there was nothing to discuss, and the trial commenced. Yuval pleaded guilty, adding he refused to serve 'on grounds of conscience'. In hindsight, Yuval defines his refusal as 'an act of egoism. I was of course concerned for the Palestinian detainees, but my most immediate consideration was to keep my self-respect, so I could look at myself in the mirror'.

Yuval's 'egoism' got him another 28 days in Atlit prison. As he recalls it, his imprisonment was not a painful ordeal: 'I don't suffer in such situations.' The food had improved over his previous term, when he went hungry, being unable to chew the hard meat-cakes. Once a week there was a half hour visit. His parents came, his brother and sister too. Visitors could bring food as long as it was in its original packaging. Yuval recalls talking with his mouth full, since he was forbidden to bring the remaining food into the prison; the visitors had to take it away.

Meanwhile, word of his imprisonment reached Yesh Gvul, and the group's media spokesman got Yuval's case published in *Ha'aretz*. This report was then quoted in the Palestinian *Al Quds* newspaper on 8 July, citing Yuval as declaring: 'I prefer to be in jail as a prisoner and not as the warder of political prisoners imprisoned without trial.' *Al Quds* was available to Palestinian prisoners in all Israeli jails, and the story of an (unnamed) Israeli army lieutenant who had preferred to go to prison himself, rather than serve as warder to Palestinians, caught the eye of Imad Sabi, a 35-year-old Palestinian in his twentieth month of administrative detention at the Sharon prison in central Israel on charges – never verified in court – that he was a senior militant with the Popular Front for the Liberation of Palestine. Prior to his arrest, Sabi had been head of the Bissan Institute of Research and Development, and translator at the Centre for Women's Studies at Bir Zeit university. He wrote copiously in his cell – a diary for his daughter Dina and literary pieces in Arabic and Hebrew. He had never had the chance to take up a stipend he gained to pursue his masters' studies in economics in Holland. His studies were supposed to commence in September 1996, Sabi had petitioned the army to release him from detention so he could take up his studies, but his request was turned down. Even his pledge not to visit the occupied territories for 18 months had been of no avail.

Intrigued by the report in *Al Quds*, Imad Sabi composed an open letter to the newspaper, dated : 'Sharon prison, 13 July 1997' and addressed to the 'unnamed Israeli officer'.

### Imad Sabi's letter

*Who are you? Who are you, officer?*

*I want to write to you, but first I must know who you are. I must know the grounds that induced you to act as you did. I must know how you reached that decision of principle, of conscience; how did you take up that rebellion, so unique, so unexpected?*

*Who are you?*

*What is your name? Where do you live? What is your profession? How old are you? Do you have children? Do you like the sea? What books do you read? What are you doing at this moment in the cell where you are incarcerated? Do you have enough cigarettes? Is there anybody there who agrees with you? Do you ask yourself: 'Was it worth paying this price?' What feelings fill your soul, trapped between the bare walls closing in on you? Do I know you? Have we ever met?*

*Can you see the moon and stars from your cell window? Have your ears grown used to the jangling of the heavy keys, the squeaking of locks, the banging of iron doors? What was said to you at your trial, what did you reply? In your sleep, do you see wheat fields and sheaves swaying in the wind? Do you see fields of sunflowers, your eyes filled with the shades of yellow, green, black … and the sun scorching you, you smile in your sleep, the cells walls tumble and collapse, and a stranger waves at you from a distance.*

*Who are you, lieutenant? Why do you attach such importance to the matter of administrative detention?*

*Please, tell me, who are you? Is my freedom really so important to you? .*

*Would the role of warder really break you down? Just a week, or two or three at most, and you'd complete your reserve duty and go back to your civilian life. You could have remained silent, controlled your anger, kept your feelings to yourself, been a polite warder, treated the detainees courteously, tactfully, humanely. What would have happened if you had behaved like that?*

*So who are you?*

*How do the warders treat you? Does your wife visit you – or maybe your girlfriend, your mother, your children? Do you write letters? To whom? How do you commence a letter to a woman you love? Do you think of me? What is the significance of my freedom to you? What is the significance of freedom overall, in your eyes? Isn't 'national security' of greater importance? What if I am a genuine terrorist? What would you say in that case?*

*Don't you have regrets? Didn't you entertain any doubts when they told you: 'They're dangerous, they belong to [the armed Palestinian militias] of Hamas, the Islamic Jihad, the Popular Front. Don't you trust our security police? Do you really think we imprison the innocent?'*

*So who are you?*

*Are you asleep right now? Or lying on your back, staring at the ceiling, lost in thought? What is the colour of your eyes? Are you tall or short? What makes you happy, what gets you mad? Do they allow you to receive books? Do they allow you a daily paper? What do you see in the eyes of your warders? Do you smile a lot? Do you hear the birds twitter at dawn? Do the prison blankets bother you? Will there be peace? Will the Oslo accords bring peace? Is the Likud party interested in peace? Is the Labour party interested in peace? ... Does the reality of prison resemble what you imagined?*

*Why do I feel that I know you? Have we corresponded before? I have a friend who writes against administrative detention. Is he your friend too? Do you get visits from a lady attorney? (I wrote 'lady attorney' advisedly: lady attorneys are generally more sensitive, more attentive and devoted than male attorneys.)*

*Isn't it funny to read Benyamin Netanyahu's words ... that 'a man is innocent as long as his guilt has not been established'? Indeed, is every man innocent as long as his guilt has not been established? And what about the thoughts in a man's heart? Are you sure of the man's innocence? And what about 'national security'? Why do you stir up trouble? Why are you stubborn? Why don't you act like all the others? Why do you defend persons you don't know?*

*Do you have answers to all these questions? But first tell me: who are you? Do my questions bother you, lieutenant? And why should I bother you with all these questions?*

*Unknown lieutenant, whatever your name may be, may your sleep be sweet, the tranquil sleep of a man whose conscience is clear. I shall find out your name and then I'll write you a long letter, a letter from one convict to another. I shall commence the letter with: 'Shalom, dear _____' and conclude it with: 'Yours faithfully, Imad'.*

•••

Shortly after his release from prison at the end of July 1997, Yuval was interviewed at his home by *Ha'aretz* journalist Dalia Karpel. It was she who first showed him Imad's letter (translated by Dr. Ilana Hammerman, well-known writer, translator and literary editor, and an activist in the campaign against administrative detention). The letter touched Yuval deeply and his first reaction was: 'It vindicates everything. Being in prison was worth it, in spite of everything that went with it'.

Karpel also showed Yuval a photograph of Sabi, which had been printed in *Ha'aretz* in November 1996 to illustrate a piece by journalist Gideon Levy about the incarcerated intellectual who wrote about Paul Auster, Noam Chomsky, Nelson Mandela, and missing Israeli airforce navigator Ron Arad. Having learned Hebrew in prison and undertaken a thorough study of Israeli culture, Sabi also referred to editorials from the Israeli press, quoting interviews with politicians.

Yuval was moved by the picture of Imad, taken in Ramallah in the summer of 1995 with his baby daughter Dina in his arms. Yuval's comment: 'We're both fathers of little girls, but Sabi has scarcely had a chance to see his daughter for two years'. Yuval spoke with great feeling about Imad's

Yuval Lotem and Imad Sabi

personality as reflected in the letter. 'It came from the heart. He's a man who lives and breathes the fields, dreams of freedom and of his little daughter ... a man in his prime, unafraid to express his sensitivity. That is also how he writes the letter addressed to me, fearlessly and with emotions exposed. It isn't the frenzied letter of a freedom fighter putting you on notice that he will fight without fear. Sabi presents the other side, his vulnerability and dreams.'

A week after Yuval's release, Imad's letter was published in the *Ha'aretz* weekend supplement as part of the long feature Karpel had written about the circumstances of Yuval's imprisonment. The detailed account offered Yuval an opportunity to present the reasons and circumstances behind his refusal, with particular stress on his link with an imprisoned Palestinian 'terrorist'. In later years, as heavy pressure from the military induced the Israeli media to impose a virtual blackout on the refusenik movement, such an article would have been unthinkable. But at the time, the press – the liberal *Ha'aretz* in particular – gave the refusenik issue considerable publicity, not least because of its human interest.

Yuval lost no time in writing a long letter to Imad Sabi. He also called Sabi's wife, Reem, and finally met up with her outside the Sharon prison as she came to visit her husband. Later, Reem invited Yuval to lunch at her Ramallah home, where many of Imad's friends and acquaintances also came along to see this Israeli who refused to be part of the oppressive apparatus of occupation.

Meanwhile, the feature in *Ha'aretz* aroused widespread interest, bringing the issue of administrative detainees to public attention and evoking renewed protests from human rights groups, which exerted pressure on the authorities. Imad's Israeli attorney, Tamar Peleg, had recently lodged an appeal against his continued detention. The hearing was held a few weeks later, and in spite of previous rejections, the appeal was approved. Imad was freed from prison that same day – August 26, Yuval's birthday. 'It was the best present,' he recalls, although insisting that there is absolutely no clear proof or indication that his own protest had contributed in any way to Imad's release.

Losing no time, Imad left for Holland to take up his studies, and was joined there by Reem and Dina. Yuval and Imad kept up their correspondence, occasionally speaking by phone. In January 1998, Yuval went to Europe for a brief stint in his occasional pursuit as ski instructor. Taking the opportunity, he headed for Amsterdam, to meet the Sabi family.

They were waiting for him at the railway station, along with a Dutch television crew anxious to record that first emotional meeting between the two men. The Sabis refused to hear of Yuval staying at a hotel, insisting on putting him up at their home. It was the beginning of a close and intimate association that has continued ever since. In Yuval's words, 'Imad is one of my best friends, I can talk with him about almost everything, including the most personal matters'.

Back in Israel, Yuval pursued his interest in administrative detainees, corresponding with a number of them. By some strange chance, almost every detainee he wrote to was released shortly afterwards. The story went the rounds, and families of other detainees begged him to write to their loved ones, apparently convinced that his letters bore some magic charm, though Yuval himself doubts it...

Noa Levy of the 'Shministim' (high school students who refuse to join the army of occupation) lights a torch at Yesh Gvul's now traditional Alternative Independence Day celebration, held on 6 May 2003 opposite the prime minister's office in Jerusalem.

# The Alternative Independence Day Ceremony

As part of its philosophy of all-out opposition to the official Israeli establishment, Yesh Gvul maintains a tradition of holding its own 'alternative' celebration of Israel's Independence Day, just a kilometre from the official event. In a parody of the official torch-lighting ceremony, which honours privileged personages favoured by the establishment, the Yesh Gvul ceremony grants a similar honour to representatives of the under-privileged, the poor, the disabled, feminists, human rights advocates and the Palestinian minority in Israel. The following advertisement heralded the 1998 ceremony:

---

Yesh Gvul will mark Israel's 50th Independence Day with an
**ALTERNATIVE TORCH-LIGHTING CEREMONY**
to be held at Emil Gruenzweig Square, opposite the prime minister's office, on Wednesday April 29 1998 at 7:30 p.m

While official ceremonies omit all mention of the **true** issues surrounding Independence Day, the **protest ceremony** will kindle torches to commemorate:
- the government's efforts to demolish the peace process;
- the unemployed and underprivileged excluded from the independence celebrations;
- the Arab minority subjected to discrimination and repression;
- sexist discrimination against women, Jewish and Arab.

The first torch will be kindled by **Shulamit Aloni**, followed by other well-known figures from the peace movement, and protest groups representing the socially and ethnically disadvantaged

---

Three years later, at the Yesh Gvul ceremony marking Independence Day 2001, torches were lit by:

**Reuven Abergil**, a founder member of the Black Panthers protest movement of Eastern Jews; **Hulud Badawi**, head of the Arab Student's Committee, Haifa University; **Neta Golan**, peace activist, recently arrested in Hares village (West Bank) for protecting olive trees; **Ilan Galon**, Knesset member of the Meretz party, active in legislation for the handicapped; **Yoav Hass**, Yesh Gvul activist, jailed for refusal; **Salem Jubran**, Palestinian Israeli poet and writer; **Dalia Kershtein**, director of the Hotline for Defence of the Individual; **Noam Kuzar**, army conscript recently jailed for refusing to serve in the occupied territories; **Moshe Negbi**, journalist and jurist, recently fired from the daily *Ma'ariv* for defying its proprietor; **Haya Shalom**, activist in Israel's homo-lesbian movement; **Dan Yakir**, legal advisor to the Israeli Society for Civic Rights.

# The Second *Intifada*

The second Palestinian uprising, or *intifada*, erupted in September 2000, following the collapse of the peace process and in response to a long series of Israeli provocations. These culminated in the controversial visit by then opposition politician Ariel Sharon to the Islamic shrine in Jerusalem, the Dome of the Rock. The Israeli army had long prepared for the confrontation with a series of measures that included training combat units for assaults on Palestinian villages. The repression was infinitely more brutal than in the first *intifada*, with Israeli troops instructed to use live gunfire against Palestinian protesters usually armed with nothing more than stones. As the conflict flared up, Palestinians too resorted to their guns, whereupon the Israeli command committed tanks, helicopters and combat planes. A wave of Palestinian suicide bombings, mainly directed at Israeli civilians, heightened the ferocity of the standoff and united the majority of Israelis around the official campaign of repression.

Up to the second *intifada*, the overwhelming majority of refuseniks were reservists called in for a few weeks of annual service. Conscripts rendering their standard three years of compulsory service were usually too overawed by the strict discipline to which they were subjected, and only a mere handful showed any resistance. That is not to say that young soldiers involved in the fighting did not suffer severe pangs of conscience. Their moral dilemma had been presented, with bitter irony, in a letter one young conscript had written to a newspaper in February 1988, during the first *intifada*. Dov Barak had continued to do military service in the occupied territories.

# Letter to the editor of *Koteret Rashit* from Dov Barak

*In all the difficult predicaments, in every war, a faithful individual is expected to risk his life, and render it up, for values. All the struggles our people has gone through in the battle for its very survival, its right to exist on an equal basis with other nations, the struggle by Jews to be considered human and live as such – have taken their bloody toll. The military authorities are authorised to order you to waive your humanity during wartime, and to become a machine; you become a machine, as does the enemy you face. It is exclusively in the army, during wartime, that human consciousness is capable of denying itself.*

*A short break; ladies and gentlemen are invited to sip coffee and nibble cake, for the introduction will be followed by the denouement: awareness.*

*I, a proud young Jew, nineteen last summer, want to tell you about what you call 'an iron fist', or 'application of reasonable force' This isn't a televised 'report from the occupied territories' or 'weekly diary'. It's an attempt to tell you what passes through my mind under my steel helmet and behind the defensive uniform.*

*The heavy club in my right hand, my Galil assault rifle in the left, and I, like my fellow-conscripts, keep order, enforce the curfew. Carry out my superiors' orders and those of authority. I stand behind the newspaper report that 'order has been restored in the Palestinian refugee camps'.*

*Sip your coffee, it's getting cold, take another bite of cake, light a cigarette. Don't worry: you might be indignant, maybe hope and pray; but I'm here, beating, carrying out my orders to the letter, and gradually going crazy.*

*Like everything else in the IDF, the club too can be divided into three parts: the fist, the club and the head. At the first blow – I recall it was at a woman's shoulder – I was horrified, I shut my eyes and prayed in my heart for her not to feel the blow, that it would evaporate in some miraculous manner, that I wouldn't harm her. In time, I learned the lingo: blocking blow, direct blow, limb-breaking blow – all of them 'reasonable' blows. After intensive drilling, I developed the required skills: for a blow that breaks anything, you have to raise the club in a circular movement, two thirds of the length of the target with the desired force – that makes it 'reasonable'.*

*Curfew at the Herpa refugee camp. All is deserted; no-one is outside, only soldiers and dogs. Suddenly a kid crosses the road: he may resemble your child, at a run. Curfew is curfew and orders are orders. Beatings are a matter of routine, but in this instance, how irritating, my consciousness awoke to* declare: '*A child is a child. Even if he's a warmonger and a little son-of-a-bitch, he's a child.*' *My destructive consciousness, fruit of years of humanitarian upbringing, took up a defensive posture, enfolding and protecting the child, in order also to protect itself with all its might. But I'm a soldier, I'm obedient, and I raise the club.*

*With trained blows and employing reasonable force, I demolish consciousness. When my consciousness is destroyed, I discover myself no longer human but a wild animal, and recall Jewish history 45 years back, as I stand there in uniform and steel helmet, with club and rifle but no consciousness. The kid is loaded on a truck to be taken to hospital, and the curfew is enforced.*

•••

In its bid to crush the second *intifada*, the army command flung a new generation of 18-year-old soldiers into a bitter confrontation with the Palestinian population. For a brave handful of youngsters, the horrors surrounding the campaign of repression helped break the pattern of compliance prevalent hitherto among the young recruits. Familiar, like most Israelis, with the refusenik movement, a group of high school students (*shministim* i.e. pupils of the top class) awaiting induction wrote a joint letter to prime minister Ariel Sharon, putting him on notice that they would not take part in the campaign of repression. Published initially with 62 signatures, it snowballed into a massive protest, and the number of signatories soon rose to over 300. When the time came for their induction, the youngsters backed words with deeds. Numbers of them refused to don uniform, and were subjected by the military authorities to savage retribution aimed at breaking their spirits.

# Letter from the *Shministim*\*
## to prime minister Ariel Sharon

We the undersigned, youths who grew up and were brought up in Israel, are about to be called to serve in the IDF. We protest before you against the aggressive and racist policy pursued by the Israeli governments and its army, and to inform you that we do not intend to take part in the execution of this policy.

We strongly resist Israel's pounding of human rights. Land expropriation, arrests, executions without trial, house demolition, closure, torture, and denial of health care are only some of the crimes the state of Israel carries out, in flagrant violation of international conventions it has ratified.

These actions are not only illegitimate; they do not even achieve their stated goal – increasing the citizens' personal safety. Such safety will be achieved only through a just peace agreement between the Israeli government and the Palestinian people.

Therefore we will obey our conscience and refuse to take part in acts of oppression against the Palestinian people, acts that should properly be called terrorist actions. We call upon persons our age, conscripts, soldiers in the standing army, and reserve service soldiers to do the same.

Signed by:

| | |
|---|---|
| *Haggai Matar,* | *Reut Katz,* |
| *Yair Hilo,* | *Yoni Cohen,* |
| *Sahni Werner,* | *Amir Melanki,* |
| *Neta Zalmanson,* | *Uriah Oren,* |
| *Ra'anan Forschner,* | *Tali Lerner and others* |
| *Matan Kaminer,* | |

---

\* Pupils of the top class in high school

# STATEMENTS BY JAILED CONSCRIPTS

## Those who enlist and those who don't
### Uri Yaakovi

*18-year-old Uri Yaakovi sent the following letter to the daily* **Ha'aretz** *on 18 August 2002, two days ahead of his enlistment date. He did indeed refuse to enlist and was jailed. Earlier, Yaakovi had been an active member of the* **Shministim** *group of high school students who wrote to Sharon.*

Two days from now, I won't enlist. I'll get on the bus with the other inductees and after we get off at the intake base I, unlike the rest, will refuse to be conscripted, and I'll probably get sent to prison where I'll encounter my colleagues of the *Shministim* letter. They, like many others, have grasped that the campaign Israel is conducting in the occupied territories – like many other wars in the course of history – is not the 'war of the sons of light against the sons of darkness'.

When we hear on the foreign media that Israeli tanks are thundering through the streets of Palestinian cities (for some reason we rarely get to hear this in the Israeli media) we don't hear the whole truth. The sad truth is that what the IDF does in the occupied territories goes beyond tanks demolishing the civilian infrastructure, or soldiers at road blocks delaying women in childbirth or just plain callousness towards Palestinian civilians. Our soldiers find themselves in difficult predicaments; some also make mistakes. But they kill children and old people who certainly are unconnected to any terrorist activity, demolish the homes of entire families and commit other actions best defined as 'terrorism'. All these actions are unforgivable, and I refuse to take a hand therein. There is no justice in them, no reason in the world – certainly not the wish to colonise another stretch of land – that makes them morally correct, just as attacks on Israeli civilians are neither correct nor moral.

I don't know whether the Palestinian leadership seeks peace. I don't know whether the Palestinians want to remain forever impoverished and disadvantaged (though I find it hard to believe they do). I just know that the Palestinians don't want us as their occupiers. I know they don't want to live in combat and witness the continued bloodshed. I know it isn't them who force us to occupy them; we do it very well without their assistance.

I am not proud of my people, I am not proud of my state, I am not proud of the actions being carried out on behalf of my security, I am not even proud that I'm about to go to jail over my refusal to serve in this army of occupation (and I'm not even overjoyed at being given the opportunity to suffer for my convictions). I am proud of being attentive to the voice of my conscience, and I shall be delighted if others are attentive to theirs, rather than to what they are told by their commanding officers.

# Militarism and racism have reached a fascist level

## Haggai Matar

*Haggai Matar, who comes from a family of political activists, was a leading light in the group of* **Shministim** *who wrote to Sharon and other ministers putting them on notice that they will take no part in the repression in the occupied territories. Matar issued his statement on the day of his induction, which was also the date of his imprisonment for refusal to enlist.*

Today, 23 October 2002, I will be sent to the military prison, as a result of my insistence upon my political views, which prevent me from enlisting in the IDF.

Despite my young age, merely 18, and despite the fact that I do not bear with me memories from Israel's past, I can wholeheartedly declare that Israel has reached an unprecedented moral low. This extreme deterioration began with 'Barak's generous offers', which were but another attempt at forcing a unilateral agreement upon the Palestinian people. Today, militarization and racism among the Jewish population have reached a fascist level. The repression of critical thinking, the total acceptance of the occupation's crimes, the idolization of the army and the gradual acceptance of the principle of 'ethnic cleansing' – all these constitute only part of our society's collapse. To this list one should add the systematic mistreatment of the Palestinian citizens of Israel, the hateful violence addressed at peace demonstrators, and the heartless attitude towards the abnormal and the weak. *With all these, I refuse to cooperate.*

The voice of conscience and the lessons humanity should have learnt from countless similar situations in the past *leave me no choice* but to refuse enlistment to the Israeli army – which is falsely dubbed a 'Defence Force'. My refusal to enlist is inevitable. The oppression known by the peoples of this area in the age of the Empires, the torment of the slaves and the Indians in North America, the Algerian War of Independence and *apartheid* in South Africa – all these precedents have made my refusal inevitable. My grand-father's actions in the Second World War, in his fight against Nazi Fascism, and his belief in humanism – these too lead to my refusal. At home I learnt of oppression and justice. In the face of such evil as one may find here and now, there is no other way.

On this significant day of my life, accompanied by my supportive family and friends, I wish to acknowledge my companions, the unseen heroes of our struggle: the Palestinian who endures the occupation without turning to violence against the Israeli civilian population, in spite of his lack of hope for a decent life; the Palestinian citizen of Israel, who keeps striving for co-existence despite day-to-day humiliations; the youth who avoids serving the occupation, her upbringing notwithstanding; the European peace activist, who physically defends Palestinians in the Occupied Territories; and my friend, a girl raised in a right-wing family, who fell in love with an Arab and was consequently banished from her home. While in prison, when forced to salute State and Army, I shall, in my mind and heart, be saluting all my brave friends, whom I cannot equal, because of my identity; all those who sacrifice so much more then I do – for peace, against the occupation.

## I am a prisoner, yet free

### A letter to his parents by David Haham-Herson

All the terrible reports appearing daily in the press, I read here in Military Jail 4. No pictures, no soundtrack. I see only barbed wire fences, but the pain from outside goes deep. Revenge in return for revenge, killing in return for killing. Why, I ask, does the Jewish people generate so much suffering, why do we inflict – on others and ourselves – so much pain? What is the source of the Israeli sense of pride, why is the act of killing considered so great in our eyes?

I am a soldier in the Israeli army, imprisoned for refusal to take part in repression, arising from a sense that it is out of the question to be a Jew, the son of a people of refugees, and yet repress a people of refugees (there's no disagreement in the Israeli public regarding repression of the Palestinians, merely over whether or not it's justified). I am a God-fearing Jew, and as such forbidden to take part in denying freedom and serving in occupied territory. I am imprisoned, but yet feel freer than most of the Israelis I've met, for one simple reason: I don't bear the burden of vindictiveness and the perverse gratification attending it. I don't bear the burden of denial and callousness. I am concerned for humans as such. For those denied the right to live like me, with food and clothes and fun and good health and dreams of success and a car. I am concerned for people who are humiliated every day, who are denied the right to work, who are imprisoned within their towns and villages. I am concerned for those whose homes have been demolished and their fruit groves devastated.

I am concerned because I know that the terrible hatred towards me is justified. This hatred has led to horrifying and perverted manifestations, like the young suicide bombers, but we create the conditions that lead to this monstrosity. I am concerned because I know that the cries of exultation over the killings drown out the sobs of the numerous victims, Jews and Arabs, of the widows and orphans, of the cripples who will suffer for the rest of their lives because of that pride and callousness.

This is a concern unlike that of most of the Israeli people. For this concern demands correction (*tikkun*) whereas the other concern merely calls for more destruction. I am a prisoner yet free, but the pain runs deep. I hope my imprisonment, and that of others, will lead many in our society to contemplation – contemplation of the Palestinians, and by way of them, contemplation of ourselves. I regard my imprisonment as the true way to participate in present day Israeli society. I don't think my imprisonment releases me from responsibility. Even if I weren't serving in the army, I'd continue to share responsibility for these actions. I'm not the victim. On the contrary: precisely because I regard myself as sharing responsibility, I refuse to take part in the repression.

I am a soldier and wish to serve my country. I am a part of Israeli society: that is where I find people I love, including some who act contrary to my convictions. They include right and left. I just want us Israelis – strong, triumphant – to look into the eyes of those we repress, and try to understand them. For the victory of might is no victory. Our fears will leave us only when we consent to equality between peoples and between individuals. We too shall continue to live in fear as long as we implement oppression and deny elementary rights.

Instead of justifying suffering – that which we inflict, and our own – we should try to solve it by self correction (*tikkun atzmi*). Faith in *tikkun* is a weapon more powerful than tanks. I regard my imprisonment as a foundation for *tikkun*, and hope that by way of thinking about it, others will look at the reality about us, and contribute to change.

# A violent and racist society

**Itamar Shahar**

I the undersigned, Itamar Shahar (Military ID 7015540), hereby declare that I am no longer willing to continue to serve in the IDF. The actions the army has been conducting these past two years in the West Bank and Gaza Strip are immoral and non-legitimate. Injuring and killing hundreds of innocent civilians; denying medical attention, education and a livelihood to millions of human beings; actions of deportation, demolishing homes and uprooting fruit groves – these are deeds which cannot be tolerated, certainly one cannot take part therein or in the body perpetrating them. The Israeli government's policy of occupation, repression and colonisation is the cause of the bloodshed in our region, whose principal casualties are civilians on both sides. Accordingly, if we wish to live a dignified, free and peaceful existence here, we must fight the occupation that brings calamity upon both peoples, and refuse to carry out any action that serves to perpetuate the occupation.

In my view, the state of Israel, like any other state, has the right to maintain a popular armed force to be deployed in defence of the lives of the state's citizens, when there are no alternatives available. Possessing the ability and the willingness to contribute to this army, I enlisted in August 2000 for combat service in the IDF. Two months after my induction, at the end of September 2000, violence erupted in the Gaza Strip and West Bank. Since then, I have served many months in the bloc of Jewish settlements in the Gaza Strip known as the 'Katif Bloc'.

In the course of those months, I made a close acquaintance with the daily reality of occupation: the humiliating delays and searches at road blocks; the deplorable exploitation of Palestinian workers by the Jewish settlers who took their land; the settlers who are willing to neglect the physical and psychological wellbeing of their children for material gain or out of funda- mentalist religious conviction; the callousness of the military authorities towards the needs of the Palestinian population thrown upon their mercies; and the psychological change undergone by 18-year-old youngsters suddenly granted the power to dominate other human beings. It is precisely this close acquaintance that has led me to conclude that it is out of the question to behave in a moral manner in circumstances founded upon the relationship between occupier and occupied. Initially, I thought it might be possible to try and improve these circumstance to a degree, but ultimately I understood that the only way for an ordinary soldier to defend the wellbeing of all concerned, Palestinians and Israelis, is by refusing to take a hand in the occupation apparatus.

After talking the matter over with my superiors, and after a number of months during which I was not assigned any duties, I was posted to serve as instructor of the intelligence section at a basic training camp in the Negev. Naively, I believed that this duty would be confined to contributing to the defence of the citizens of Israel, and I was overjoyed at being given duties that would perhaps enable me to influence the outlook of young soldiers commencing their military service. But I soon learned that even this task constitutes direct assistance to the occupation apparatus.

In April 2002, shortly before being posted to my new assignment, the Israeli army commenced – on instructions from the government – a series of barbaric attacks on Palestinian population centres in the West Bank, entailing violation of all the most basic moral norms as expressed not merely in international conventions, but also in the laws of the state of Israel and the ethical code of the IDF itself. Even in war, there are rules that may not be violated. In April 2002, the gravest of war crimes were committed, not only by ordinary soldiers in the field, but also by senior officers and the political echelons, the latter handing down to the combat units orders that were flagrantly illegal. These events further exacerbated the doubts and perplexities bearing upon me: how could I be in the ranks of a body, a considerable portion of whose present actions constitute terrorism against innocent civilians?

The name of the operation – 'Defensive Wall' – was a cover for the systematic demolition of the physical and human infrastructure of Palestinian civilian society, simultaneously destroying any hope of reconciliation between the two peoples in the foreseeable future. Now that on the Palestinian side of the green line nothing is left but physical destruction and human beings who are demoralised, hungry and oppressed, Sharon can easily prove his claims that the other side is 'no partner for peace'.

My act of refusal is not entirely altruistic: I am not refusing merely over the violation of the human rights of the people of the West Bank and Gaza – even though in my view those are perfectly adequate grounds – but also for the benefit of Israeli society, in which I live. The destinies of the two peoples are interconnected, and the harm inflicted upon the Palestinians prompts some of them to adopt non-legitimate measures of harming innocent citizens of Israel, so that fear has become a central component of our routine existence. Thirty-five years of occupation have made Israeli society violent and racist, a society wherein many live in poverty and ignorance. As though that were not sufficient, we are destroying the last lingering chance of achieving peace in this region. If we do not sober up, as members of the dominant nation, to allow the Palestinian people to achieve its legitimate rights, we shall find ourselves in an even worse plight than that which we have reached.

In my view, a decent moral person will consent to serve in the national army on two basic conditions:

(a) The army shall serve exclusively to defend the lives and liberty of the state's citizens, and no other purpose

(b) The state and its security agencies shall, in all their actions, observe a basic moral code arising out of the equal value of all human beings, as expressed in international conventions such as the Geneva Convention for the Protection of Civilians in Wartime and the Universal Declaration of Human Rights.

In view of the gross violation of these conditions by the Israeli government and its army, and in view of the fact that any assignment with the IDF entails assistance to immoral and non-legitimate policies which bring disaster upon the entire region, I hereby declare that, as of this week, I no longer regard myself as an IDF soldier obliged to comply with military orders. The moment the aforementioned conditions are fulfilled adequately, I shall be willing to place myself at the disposal of any service required for the citizens of the state in which I live.

# STATEMENTS BY JAILED RESERVISTS

## Declaration of refusal

*Along with the startlng adherence of young conscripts to the refusal movement, the second* intifada *soon produced its crop of reservist refuseniks, whose numbers grew rapidly. Soon after the* intifada *began, Yesh Gvul collected the signatures of hundreds of reservists on the following petition:*

Despite a semblance of Palestinian autonomy (on no more than a fifth of the occupied territories) the occupation goes on and on. Over thirty years of occupation and repression have not halted the Palestinian struggle for national independence.

The war prosecuted by the Israeli government – in defence of the settlements of Ariel and Bethel, of the thugs of Itamar and Beit Hadassah in Hebron, for continued occupation of Netzarim and Kiryat Arba, and continued control of Rachel's Tomb in Bethlehem and Nebi Samuel – is not OUR war.

We the undersigned, IDF soldiers, declare that we will not take part in the continued oppression of the Palestinian people in the occupied territories, and will not take a hand in the policing and defence of the settlements serving that end.

## Vile injustice

**David Enoch**

*A lieutenant in the reserves, David Enoch was sentenced to 25 days' jail for refusing to serve in the Ramallah area.*

My commitment to the principles of justice, honesty and fairness – which lay behind the decisions that shaped my military service – is now the cornerstone of the decision for which I am being penalised. I don't find that systematic denial of human rights to hundreds of thousands of persons is in keeping with basic moral principles, and I therefore refuse to take part therein.

Any thoughtful person sets out – or should set out – lines he will not cross, even if it is demanded by ostensibly valid orders. The vile injustice arising from unjust denial of human rights to hundreds of thousands lies far beyond that line.

## The red line

### Michael Sfard

*A sergeant in the reserves, Sfard was sentenced to 21 days' jail for refusing to serve as escort for Israeli settlers in the occupied territories. Sfard is now an attorney active in civil rights cases. He recently petitioned the Israeli Supreme Court on behalf of refusenik David Zonsheine against the army's rejection of Zonsheine's demand to be tried by court-martial. Zonsheine claims he can only defend his action before a properly constituted court, rather than by the disciplinary procedure the army prefers for such cases. The petition is pending.*

I didn't want to refuse an order. I didn't look forward to that moment. If there were any way it could have been avoided, I think I would have chosen it. It's no fun to refuse, it isn't heroic. When you're in prison, you don't constantly think, 'I'm right and the others are wrong'. On the contrary, you think, 'Maybe I'm wrong and the others are right'. You're consumed with doubt.

But sometimes there's no alternative to refusal. That 'no alternative' hits each person at a different moment. That is the personal aspect of refusal. My 'red line' isn't always yours, and vice versa. But for both of us, crossing that line is giving up your personality, your uniqueness, your values and above all, your conscience. I wouldn't refuse every order to serve in the occupied territories. But I was ordered to do three weeks of guarding settlers; my duties would include body searches on passing Palestinians, and arrests when necessary. Were I to do that, I would no longer be the same person.

# We won't take part!

*A Yesh Gvul leaflet distributed to IDF soldiers at bus stations and military transportation locations during the early months of the second intifada.*

**We won't take part**
- in a siege that deprives civilians of food, schooling and medical care;
- in a war over the settlements of Netzarim, Kfar Darom, Kiryat Arba and Psagot – a war that kills women, men, children and babies.

**That war is not our war !!!**
Soldier, bear in mind:
- The Fourth Geneva Convention outlaws collective punishment, intimidation, terror or reprisals against civilians or their property.
- The Convention forbids infliction of physical suffering, torture, maiming or murder of civilians.
- The Occupying Power must refrain from subjecting the occupied population to physical or moral coercion.
- The Occupying Power must protect the inhabitants of the occupied territory from violence, threats or humiliation.

(Appendix 61 to High Command Orders, collation of legal opinions no. 8, 1977, HQ of the Military Attorney General, 1979, p. 127.)

**Are you ready to have your children or grandchildren ask you if you took part in war crimes?**

Remember!
An Israeli court found – 40 years ago – that a soldier is forbidden to obey a flagrantly illegal order. Don't take the risk of allowing some judge to find that you shared in carrying out such an order.

Remember!
The international community has recently indicted soldiers who committed war crimes in Serbia, Bosnia, Uganda, Chile and elsewhere. The sentences ran to long years of imprisonment. Would you want to risk it?

There are instructions, orders and duties that are 'legal' but immoral.

The legislature, acting on ideological or pragmatic grounds, has legalised such flagrantly immoral acts. But is it moral in your eyes to subject a woman in labour to endless delay at a road block?

Is it moral in your eyes to conduct a body search on a woman who has just given birth at the road block, with the baby still attached to her by the umbilical cord? Is it moral in your eyes to deny treatment to cancer patients? Is it moral in your eyes to deny food and water supplies to Palestinian towns and villages? Is it moral in your eyes to prevent hundreds of thousands of Palestinians from earning a decent living?

Is it moral in your eyes to repress the 1.5 million Palestinians of the Gaza Strip, merely to meet the whims of the 5,000 Jewish settlers of Gush Katif ?

**Dear soldier, there are things – even if termed 'legal' – that decent people don't do! A decent person doesn't demolish homes, or kill children, women and babies, or starve a neighbouring people or deny proper medical treatment to individuals just like me and you.**

'[When it comes] to the Hague International Court, Sharon will arrive there without me' (Transport minister Ephraim Sneh, *Yediot Aharonot*, 20/4/01). What about you, soldier?

**What can you do?**
We don't have a 'surefire recipe'. Make up your own mind, follow your conscience, your heart and mind.

We won't decide in your place. We can only tell you that there have been very many soldiers – during the Lebanon war, the first intifada and the current uprising, conscripts and reservists – who plucked up the courage to say: NO!

Whoever decides to refuse, makes his own decision. But when he does make up his mind, he'll find us extending a helping hand and counsel, supporting and helping.

Yesh Gvul member Ilan Moradi, a refusenik himself, leaflets IDF soldiers at a military transportation centre at a football stadium in West Jerusalem. The leaflet warns soldiers against taking part in human rights abuses or war crimes against the Palestinian population in the occupied territories.

## Collaboration makes me a criminal

### Ro'i Kozlovsky

*A lieutenant in the reserves, Ro'i Kozlovsky was sentenced to 18 days' jail for refusing to guard settlements.*

The settlements constitute theft of land that isn't ours. They exist on the army's bayonets. They force the army to repress hundreds of thousands of Palestinians, and place a real obstacle on the way to peace with our neighbours – just so as to permit further colonisation by a handful of fanatics, in the name of our 'historic right to ancestral land'. This policy that takes land and rights from the Arabs to give to Jews, is discriminatory, if not racist, entailing humiliation and organised violence against human beings –

Palestinians – as we see daily on TV: these acts cast a heavy shadow on every single person in Israel.

It is a basic human 'duty to refuse such reserve service. A duty that even takes precedent over the duty to obey the law of the land. Collaboration with the policy of the Israeli government makes me a criminal, for the responsibility for committing immoral acts is not merely with those who give the orders; it lies with all those ready to carry them out even though they do not agree with them.

# A cause which is not mine

### Alex Lyakas

*A student of computer science from Haifa, Alex Lyakas comes from a family of immigrants from Lithuania in the former Soviet Union. An IDF reserve sergeant, Lyakas served 24 days in Military Jail 4 in July–August 2001, for refusing to serve in the occupied territories. Lyakas likewise rejected any form of indirect aid to the current campaign of repression against the Palestinian people – as when his superiors offered a compromise whereby he was to do his reserve duty within pre-1967 Israel, cooking meals for the units in action in the territories. In a letter to his superiors, he set out his reasons for refusal:*

I am not prepared to participate in taking human lives, violating freedoms or other natural rights, as I believe is being done today in the West Bank and Gaza. Recalling the hopes surrounding my emigration to Israel, I didn't expect that in a free country I would be required to participate in actions that I so deeply oppose. I'm not seeking an easy way out of military service. As a law-abiding citizen, I am not trying to avoid reserve service with medical or other excuses. I am honestly expressing my reasons, and informing you that I cannot abandon my studies in order to be recruited for a cause which is not mine.

# 'Courage to Refuse' declaration

*In January 2002, the group of reservists that came to be known as 'Courage to Refuse' published the following proclamation. The initial publication bore 52 signatures, specifying the signatories' reserve rank (ranging from first sergeant to major) and combat unit (paratroops, armour, engineers, artillery, navy, military intelligence, airforce, Golani brigade, Givati brigade, Nahal brigade). The number of signatories is now in excess of 500.*

We, being officers and soldiers in the combat reserves of the Israel Defence Force, having been brought up on Zionism, self-sacrifice and contribution to the Israeli people and the state of Israel, having always served in the front line, having always been the first to carry out any mission, easy or difficult, to defend and buttress the state of Israel;

We, combat officers and soldiers who serve the state of Israel for many weeks each year, regardless of the heavy personal cost, have rendered reserve service throughout the occupied territories and received orders and instructions that had nothing to do with the security of the state, and whose sole purpose is perpetuation of our domination of the Palestinian people;

We, having witnessed with our own eyes the bloody toll that the occupation takes on both sides of the divide;

Who have sensed how the orders we receive erode every value we have imbibed in this country;

Who understand today that the price of the occupation is loss of the humane image of the IDF and corruption of the entire Israeli society;

Who know that the territories are not Israel, and that the Jewish settlements there will ultimately have to be evacuated;

We hereby declare that *we will no longer fight in the war for the welfare of the settlements in the territories.* We will not continue to fight beyond the Green Line [Israel's pre-1967 border] for the purpose of dominating, expelling, starving and humiliating an entire people.

We hereby declare that we will continue to serve in the Israel Defence Force in any assignment that will serve the defence of the state of Israel. *The assignment of occupation and repression does not serve that aim – and we will have no part in it.*

# An enormous 'black flag'

## Avner Kochavi

*A first sergeant with an infantry unit, Avner Kochavi is a signatory on the Courage to Refuse declaration.*

Ever since my friends learned that I've signed the declaration 'Courage to Refuse', they argue with me, telling me I should do my reserve duty, I always have the right to refuse an order that comes in the category of 'the black flag of illegality'. But those who make the claim don't understand that all the army's actions in the Palestinian territories fall into the 'black flag' category.

Let me take an example familiar to any soldier who has served in the occupied territories: a lookout post is set on the roof of a Palestinian family home. That may not sound particularly 'black flag', but I remember the first such lookout post I helped man in the town of Halhul, near Hebron.

First of all, the house walls were black with coffee grounds that the soldiers regularly emptied out from the roof. The courtyard was full of human excrement and toilet paper, because it served the soldiers as their toilet. The roof was littered with piles of garbage and tins of preserves.

The armoured truck that brought each rota squad of soldiers had smashed up the sidewalk at the entrance to the house. Whenever there was a change of guard at 2 in the morning, it woke the whole household, and the baby would start crying.

I remember the looks I got from members of the family whenever I ran into them on the stairway: the look of humiliation.

Ostensibly, there was no 'black flag' over that situation, but an enormous black flag envelops everything the army does in the midst of the Palestinian civilian population.

# A letter to the commander of Battalion 719

## Ehud Shem Tov

*A first sergeant with an armour unit and a signatory on the 'Courage to Refuse' declaration.*

I wish to explain why I will not join the battalion on its next tour of duty.

I have done my annual reserve duty with the battalion for over 16 years, I have never missed one tour, whether for training or active combat duty, I am the battalion's oldest medic. During my service I have tended the unit's dead and wounded, and, of course, casualties among the local population, Jewish and Arab.

As a young man I adopted a moral code of humane values, and that made me persist in my duty as medic. My oath was constantly before my eyes, whenever I had a hard time as a conscript and later as a reservist.

Although the actions of the Israeli government and the IDF in the occupied territories are remote from my personal outlook (I stress again: moral values, nothing political) I believed that my duty to serve with the reserves was beyond debate.

What enabled my service in the occupied territories hitherto was the conviction that my presence had a cooling influence and persuaded those about me, who are less sensitive, more raucous, more destructive, more racist, more violent, more brutal, more trigger-happy, to behave with greater moderation. I sensed that my presence helped induce more proper conduct in entering Palestinian homes, in searching their cars, in reducing the bullying of innocent civilians at road blocks, in moderating the aggressive response to demonstrations, and reducing the situations from which it was impossible to extricate ourselves without gunfire.

My last tour of duty (August–September 2001) in the Nablus sector left a painful impression on me, proving that matters had changed and my influence was now non-existent. Tanks, planes and helicopters bomb civilian towns; soldiers abuse Palestinian civilians; house searches leave behind havoc, even though everybody knows the search could be conducted in a different manner...

Let me detail some incidents from that tour of duty, incidents that helped me make up my mind to refuse service in the occupied territories as long as current circumstances persist. These incidents are testimony that I cannot continue to serve while adhering to the moral values on which I was raised in the army as soldier and medic.

## Incident 1
My second day in the sector, the battalion ambulance (the battalion doctor and three medics, including me) was alerted to an incident at the Tapuah road junction. The drive was slow because the vehicle was armoured. On the way, we were overtaken by two ambulances belonging to the Jewish settlers and additional military vehicles. When we arrived on the scene, it transpired that settlers had attacked a Red Crescent ambulance and other Palestinian vehicles. One of the drivers had lost control, his car was over-

turned and lay at the roadside, four injured Arabs lay on the ground. The Red Crescent ambulances had had their windshields smashed (the settlers had done so in a bid to delay them) and their crews were not permitted to approach the injured. There were military vehicles around, and senior officers (captains and colonels) including medical officers. I was amazed to discover that nobody was caring for the injured! One was gravely injured and required emergency treatment ... ultimately his death was determined. The version put out on the media was entirely different from what actually happened on the ground ('Arabs had thrown stones at other Arabs in an attempt to frame the Jewish settlers, Arabs snatched the body ...'). This version from the IDF spokesman was later corrected. I also remember that medics from brigade headquarters photographed the wounded Palestinians, chuckling and laughing, though claiming the photos were for documentation and study purposes. That painful picture of injured on the ground, army units about and nobody extending assistance, the IDF spokesman's statement and the conduct of the brigade medics, remained etched in my mind, proving that something had gone badly wrong.

## Incident 2

On the hill over the Jewish settlement of Bracha, above the city of Nablus, there is an IDF position that looks out on the city. In the course of that tour of duty I was astonished to discover that, every night, we were firing off bursts of automatic fire, without aiming, downhill towards inhabited houses on the city outskirts – just because we had heard firing (sometimes just a single shot) in the night. Instructions were to blast off massive fire, to make whoever was shooting stop, or to scare him. In fact, our massive response only encouraged him. I was again astonished to discover how rules of engagement (on opening fire) are given a new interpretation. None of us was in mortal danger, the shots fired at us were ineffective, and our response was aggressive, ineffective but devastating for the innocent civilians residing on the hillside – they were the only casualties.

## Incident 3

The entrance gate to brigade HQ and the walls around the camp are sprayed with slogans proclaiming 'Death to the Arabs!', 'No Arabs, no terror attacks' and similar racist slogans. I was astonished to see senior officers come and go indifferent to the slogans. By contrast, I could recall times when my reserve service was as 'clean-up cop'. During the first *intifada*, we'd raid Palestinian homes in towns and refugee camps, hauling out their residents in the middle of the night, and ordering them to erase 'inflammatory' slogans (support for the PLO or against the Jews) sprayed on house walls, not to mention a Palestinian flag hanging at some street corner, which they were required to take down and burn. I ask myself, whatever happened to the commanders who gave instructions to erase slogans from the walls of Arab homes? Why is it that when matters are reversed, and the walls in their own military home are covered with slogans, they don't care to have them erased?

I should stress again that my decision to refuse stems from my moral values as soldier and medic, not my political views as civilian. The IDF actions in the territories currently inflict – directly or indirectly – enormous suffering on innocent Palestinian civilians. Their wounded are not treated, their ambulances are held up at checkpoints, which also delay their medical teams, hospitals are bombarded, cut-offs of supplies of water and electricity directly harm the sick and cause others to fall ill, the sick have their way to hospital treatment blocked, etc., etc. – more and more injustices too long to enumerate.

I am convinced that the moral yardsticks I adopted in the army in the past, including my medic's oath, are incompatible with these injustices.

In the light of the aforegoing, I will not join the battalion for its upcoming tour of duty.

# I killed three innocent civilians

## Idan Kaspari
*A first sergeant with the Golani brigade, Idan Kaspari is a signatory on the Courage to Refuse declaration.*

Late July 1983, I killed three persons, all over 50 and none of them armed. They were innocent civilians in an occupied land. Death overtook them suddenly, out of the arbitrary acts of soldiers of the occupation army. Death overtook them fortuitously due to profound contempt for the lives of the subject population, people who are not considered human, but as inferior creatures. I and my comrades in arms, who killed those three in cold blood, didn't intend to kill them. But at the same time, we didn't care. We didn't care about the lives of persons we didn't know, who had children, who had built homes, who got up every morning for their day's work. We murdered them without blinking an eyelid, the way you crush a passing ant.

Needless to say, none of us paid the price of our deed. No investigation was ever held, and the short de-briefing by a bespectacled officer at divisional HQ lasted precisely ten minutes. The incident happened at the northwestern road block at a sleepy Lebanese town named Suq al Gharb. We were part of a mighty army that had set out to exterminate terror groups on Israel's northern borders, an army headed by a war hero and expert in exterminating terrorism, a man by the name of Ariel Sharon. Nineteen years later, both are still with us – terrorism and its exterminator – still facing off against one another, cheerfully engaging in a further bloody tango.

Terrorism is the weapon of those who have lost hope, who are humiliated and powerless. Of those who have lost faith in this world and place it in the world to come. Occupation feeds and sustains terrorism, fostering it and holding it close to its heart. Israel of recent years has defined itself by means of the occupation, by domination and humiliation of another people, and by a futile war against the terrorism generated by that hopelessness and humiliation.

Occupation is the evil spirit haunting our lives, it is the cankerous growth that dominates us, it is the abomination by which we live – we and the Palestinians, dancing our tango in an endless ocean of blood. My refusal to serve in the occupied territories is above all my cry: enough of the occupation! Enough of the daily humiliation of millions of persons, enough of following the whims and desires of a violent, unbridled cult of settlers for whom the sanctity of domination of the Other overrides any other moral or religious precept.

These people, for whom human life is worthless, have reduced the sole thing that actually exists in this world – life – to third or fourth place. That cult of colonialist settlers, brutal and self-centred, brandishes false slogans about security, Zionism and Judaism; that cult whose lies lead countless individuals – fathers, sons – to a pointless death, merely so as to preserve their colonialist-messianic fantasy. Eighty-one per cent of the world's states have recognized Israel within its green line borders. Not one – not even Micronesia (a tiny Pacific island state, regularly the only UN member to vote in support of Israel) has ever recognized Israel's hold on the territories occupied in 1967.

The claim that there is no difference between Elon Moreh (Jewish settlement established in the West Bank after the Israeli occupation in 1967) and Hanita (Jewish settlement established in the late thirties, under the British Mandatory government) is a lie and deception. Hanita was settled by Jews who had nothing but their hold on life. Elon Moreh is inhabited by sated colonialist settlers who enjoy the backing of a powerful state – until they perhaps succeed in destroying it.

Does our refusal resemble the refusal of the settlers to give up their present homes? No way! The reasons behind an action are just as important as the action itself. Our refusal stems from sanctification of life, and our recognition that it supersedes all else (the lives of all humans), and life entails living in dignity. The settlers attach supreme importance to the sanctity of the location and the soil; in effect, too, to their domination, which rests upon the humiliation of the Other. Their claims are metaphysical, but faith is a personal matter. Life, all life, is the only concrete thing we can grasp.

And of course, there's the familiar drivel: refusal is undemocratic, one should work for change from within, refusal is politically motivated etc, to which one has to reply:

(a) Democracy is not just majority rule, which in fact is its less important feature. Occupation and rule by force over the Other are undemocratic acts: they contradict democracy; they eliminate democracy; a majority decision for dictatorship is not democracy! Democracy begins with a democratic culture, and occupation is the antithesis of that culture.

(b) The moment you take part in practice in the occupation, you become part of it. The most basic way of opposing the occupation is by refusal to take part therein.

(c) Politics deal with questions of life and death, and that shouldn't be evaded. Virtually every decision we reach is a political one, so the refuse-niks are certainly a political organisation, though not a party grouping. Unfortunately, stupid journalists can't tell the difference.

On 3 July 1998, my eldest daughter was born. I didn't notice the proximity of the dates until a few weeks ago when I glanced at a diary I had kept during my military service. Fifteen years after destroying three lives, I helped create a new life. My daughter's life is the most important thing to me. I know that if I want to preserve her life, I must do everything in my power to banish death from the world, to preserve the lives of one and all. My refusal to collaborate with the occupation is part of my modest contribution to preservation of life and human dignity in this world. For life is sacred and all the rest is speculation. One should fight exclusively for life. The life of one and all. The armies of death are imbued with faith. The armies of life draw their strength from awareness.

# The shattered dream

## Omry Yeshurun

*A member of Kibbutz Yagur near Haifa, and a lieutenant with an armour unit, Omry Yeshurun is a signatory of the Yesh Gvul declaration of refusal and the parallel declaration sponsored by Courage to Refuse.*

I spent 25 years living in a dream. A wonderful dream in which I am a brave soldier defending the state of Israel from its foes. Everything was very clear in the dream – those on the other side were the bad guys, we were the good guys. I did my duty without asking questions. Certainly, living in that dream was wonderful, I gained honour and respect – I was even promoted to officer!

But then I was posted to serve in the occupied territories. The dream got a little blurred there, I'd say. It didn't take a lot of guts to hunt down Palestinian labourers slipping across the 'border' to bring food to their hungry families. But I did hunt them – in my dream, I was required to carry out my assignments to the best of my ability. In the dead of night, I entered the homes of Palestinians (their dreams were of an entirely different nature ...) and dragged young children off to the interrogation facilities of the Shabak security police. I didn't want to know what they would be dreaming of. And so the dream dragged on. I completed my military service, but I was still living my dream.

One night I had a dream. About the kid I dragged from his parents' home in the middle of the night; he pissed in his pants and wept all the way to the Para'a prison. In the morning, I wondered what that kid was doing now. And deep down inside, there was the answer, the answer I should have known long ago: that kid is now shooting at IDF roadblocks, or maybe has blown himself up with an explosive charge. Did I have a hand in that? Abruptly, I awoke from my years' long dream.

Israel, the strongest state in the Middle East, is scared that a bunch of stone-throwing kids will destroy it; and the fear is so strong we no longer look at ourselves in the mirror. We are beginning to resemble the most benighted regimes in human history: a state that sends its soldiers to break into the homes of the innocent, that places them in situations that invite bloodshed, and takes loyal care of the settlers who spit in its face; a state that sends soldiers to kill and be killed, to make it possible to continue killing and being killed.

I will no longer take part in these crimes. I will not take part in destroying the state in which I live. Enough of the occupation!

The greatest division among human beings is between those who say 'Yes' and those who say 'No'. Blessed are the no-sayers, for they shall bring the kingdom of heaven.

Yesh Gvul ad, headlined 'The Occupation – a curse on both peoples', published in *Ha'aretz* on 25 January 2000, four months into the second *intifada*. See translation opposite.

# The occupation – a curse on both peoples

*A Yesh Gvul statement, published as a paid advertisement in* Ha'aretz *in January 2002.*

Upon the Palestinians, the occupation inflicts oppression, humiliation, poverty, suffocation and despair.

On us, it incurs erosion of moral values, collapse of the economy, misery for the needy.

Both peoples are shedding their blood in a pointless struggle, entailing terrorism, assassinations and killing of the innocent.

In maintaining the occupation, the Israeli army wages war on defence-less civilians, and systematically commits unlawful acts. Its soldiers are driven to offences against Israeli and international law. The blockades and curfews on Palestinian towns fan the hatred, which prompts the next attack. **Occupation is violence, and it breeds terrorism**

The Israel Defence Force has become the Army of Defence of the settlements in the occupied territories, instead of pursuing its proper purpose – defence of the state. The occupation saps the army and its soldiers, robbing huge sums from health, education, welfare and infra-structure. Termination of the occupation will bring economic and social revival, and **allow for reduction of the term of military service and lightening the burden of reserve duty**.

Soldiers, men and women, remember:

Demolition of homes, fire at civilians, extrajudicial execution, denial of food supplies or medical treatment, denial of freedom of movement and destruction of means of livelihood – all these are immoral acts, and flagrantly illegal.

**Refuse to have any part in them!**

Since the onset of the *intifada*, hundreds of soldiers **have refused to serve in the occupied territories. Those who refused found us there, offering support and assistance.**

On Sunday 27 January, members of Yesh Gvul throughout Israel will start distributing a new leaflet to soldiers and youngsters of military age. Anyone willing to take part is urged to make contact with us.

**END THE OCCUPATION!**
**END THE BLOODSHED!**
**SHORTEN MILITARY SERVICE!**

An invitation to a 'Freedom Seder', published by Yesh Gvul in *Ha'aretz*, 1 April 2002. Held on the eve of Passover on the hillside overlooking Atlit military prison, this was the 'Seder of a Thousand Refuseniks'; the number of soldiers and reservists committed to refusing service in the occupied territories had reached four figures. See translation opposite.

# Seder of a thousand refuseniks

*An advertisement published by Yesh Gvul in April 2002, in advance of*
*the Jewish religious festival of Pesach (Passover), the traditional cele-*
*bration of the liberation of the Children of Israel from bondage in Egypt:*

*Pesach is celebrated in the Seder, a formal repast dedicated to recalling*
*the themes of enslavement and liberation, including numerous tradi-*
*tional elements of narrative, songs and prayer, including the blessings*
*over 'the four glasses of wine'. The Seder of a Thousand Refuseniks was*
*indeed held as scheduled on the hillside overlooking the military*
*prison, with all the traditional trappings and with hundreds of*
*participants from all parts of the country.*

Tuesday April 2, 2002, on the hill overlooking Military Prison 6 (Atlit),
we will hold a FREEDOM SEDER to celebrate Passover (Pesach), the
festival of freedom, in solidarity with the imprisoned refuseniks who
have offered up their own freedom in the cause of ensuring the freedom
of another people.

This will be the SEDER OF A THOUSAND REFUSENIKS, marking the fact
that the number of refuseniks – IDF soldiers and reservists who have
*already* refused to serve in the occupied territories, or are *committed* to
refusal if posted there – now runs into FOUR FIGURES.

We invite all refuseniks – past and future – to come to Atlit and join us
in raising the traditional FOUR GLASSES of freedom.

The ceremony will be held in the early afternoon, in good time to get
home before the onset of the festival.

To our friends and supporters worldwide: join us in celebrating the
Refusenik Seder with a similar event in your own community!

# The IDF teaches that it's okay to molest an Arab

## Ishai Sgi

*An artillery lieutenant of the reserves, Ishai Sgi served 26 days in prison for refusal to serve in the occupied territories. After his release he undertook a speaking tour of the United States, together with Ram Rahat of Yesh Gvul, to explain the reasons for his refusal to a wide range of audiences, Jews and non-Jews alike.*

After serving in the territories during my reserve service in December, and seeing with my own eyes the harsh injustice, and the way IDF soldiers harass anyone who's dark-skinned and speaks Arabic, I resolved I would no longer do my reserve service in the territories.

In the course of my previous tour of reserve duty, as well as from stories I heard from others in prison, I knew that IDF soldiers make a habit of halting beside Arab fruit stalls and 'taking a little something on patrol' or replenishing the store at the roadblock. They stop by fruit groves and pick watermelons and grapefruit. The Palestinian trader can only stand there and weep; after all, he doesn't want to take a beating from the soldiers, and certainly doesn't want to be shot should he object.

That's what the army teaches. That it's okay to molest an Arab, that there's no moral problem involved. Only the worst cases make it into the Israeli media, but the other incidents occur daily, everywhere and by very many soldiers. No wonder that after the instruction people receive in the army, a Druze Israeli citizen gets beaten up in a mall just because he speaks Arabic.

I served out my first term of duty in the territories. I told my superiors that as I'd already commenced my service and there was no-one to replace me, I'd complete my tour of duty – but next time I wouldn't report.

I was brought up on values that were further reinforced in the officers' course I underwent. To analyse situations involving principles, and to stand up for my beliefs. I'm sorry I didn't refuse to serve in the territories earlier, when I was a conscript or during my regular service. I see now that the things I did as a soldier were wrong, and the things soldiers do in the territories now are wrong, arising from the indoctrination we get in the army.

While serving my prison service, I requested to terminate my service with my reserve battalion. I also understood from my superiors that it would be preferable if I didn't return to the battalion again, as I'd subject the other soldiers to 'morale difficulties'.

# Black flag

### Itai Haviv

*A captain with an artillery unit and a signatory on the Courage to Refuse declaration, Itai Haviv received a 21-day sentence for refusal on 14 March 2002.*

As a combat officer in the IDF, I have served all over the West Bank and the Gaza Strip. I am not naive. There are times when you must kill in order to survive. On behalf of the state of Israel, I have chased children who threw stones at me. I have patrolled the alleyways of refugee camps. I have banged on their tin doors in the small hours of the morning. I have searched among mattresses for propaganda material. I have heard babies crying. I have hauled people out of bed to erase slogans daubed on walls. I have imposed curfews. I have dealt with Palestinian flags fluttering from power pylons. I have halted vehicles. I have confiscated identity cards. I have conveyed hand-cuffed prisoners in the back of my jeep. I have fired at rioters. I have halted hundreds of vehicles at roadblocks. I set up an outlook post on the roof of a cake shop in the main street of Gaza. The routine of occupation. Every day. Every hour. Thirty-five years.

I believed that this was a war of no-choice. After all, we had left no stone unturned in our pursuit of peace.

We have built over 100 settlements. We have sent 200,000 settlers to live there. We have lost soldiers, children, mothers. All for the sake of the security of the state. For the sake of peace. To stop the next suicide bomber. For 35 years, a black flag has flown over our heads, but we refused to see it.

No more.

# Soldier, it's in your hands!

*Part of a leaflet Yesh Gvul began distributing to IDF soldiers in the summer of 2002:*

**SOLDIER**
**We all want to defend our country.**
**We're all sick and tired of terrorism.**
**We all want peace.**
**But do our actions permit of an end to the cycle of bloodshed?**

Since 1967, Israel has ruled over 3.5 million Palestinians, running their lives by means of a forcible occupation, with continual violations of human rights.

The occupation regime has merely exacerbated Israel's security problems; at this time, it endangers the life of each one of its citizens, yours included!

**SOLDIER, it's in your hands!**

Ask yourself whether your actions in the course of your military service enhance national security. Or do those actions merely fuel the enmity and the acts of violence between us and our Palestinian neighbours?

**YOU CAN STOP THE VIOLENCE**
Even the heads of the defence establishment concede that there is no military solution to terrorism.

'All the preventative work we've done this past year is like trying to empty out the sea with a teaspoon', a senior security official admitted. (*Haaretz*, 19 December 2001)

Ami Ayalon, former head of the Shabak security police, says: 'An ideology can't be killed by killing leaders.'

**Soldier, is there a people anywhere in the world that will not resist an occupation regime?**

If you were in the Palestinians' shoes, would you be willing to bow your head to a foreign ruler?

Since the onset of the current intifada, over a thousand Israelis and Palestinians have been killed, most of them unarmed civilians taking no part in the fighting. As long as we hold on to the occupied Palestinian territories, we will continue to shed our own blood and that of the Palestinians.

# Three exercises in refusal

## Ishai Rosen-Zvi

*Reserve sergeant Ishai Rosen-Zvi served two weeks in jail in June 2001 over his refusal to take part in the campaign of oppression. At the time, he was working on his Ph.D. in Talmud studies. Rosen-Zvi cuts an unusual figure in the refusenik movement. He comes from a prominent family of religious nationalists – the community that has spearheaded the settlement drive; their unwavering adherence to concepts of the religious sanctity of the 'Promised Land' has made them into hard-core advocates of perpetuating Israel's hold on all the land 'between the River Jordan and the sea'. Rosen-Zvi's religious-nationalist convictions could have been expected to receive further reinforcement through his schooling at a* yeshivat hesder *– a religious high school whose students combine studies with military training. Such institutions are frequently hotbeds of fanatical right-wing activity, and it is extremely unusual for a graduate to adopt liberal views on the Israeli-Palestinian conflict. But as reflected in his article, Rosen-Zvi has broken the mould.*

### First round

*'You egoist ! What about your friends? After all, somebody has to do the job. Better you do it, than someone insensitive to human life.'*

There's a trap here; it has to be uncovered. Something about this argument remains entirely invisible, and therefore beyond consideration: the occupation itself. It isn't part of the story. The whole matter goes on within it: there are duties, somebody has to do the job, it can be done in a more or less decent manner, with or without sensitivity.

But there are jobs that simply must not be done, whether sensitively or not.

There are evils that are not inflicted by evil people, rather, precisely by the most highly-principled. The ones stationed at the roadblocks, the ones who don't beat the Palestinian passersby, don't curse them, don't deliberately leave them to 'dry out' in the sun. They just don't let anyone through, exactly as ordered, and thereby continue to starve and torment thousands of people. I was there in the first *intifada*, in Gaza, Tulkarem, Nablus. I was (to my shame) in Jenin two years ago. The evils are transparent. Nothing enormous. No dead babies. Just the evils that occur every moment, by your very oppressive presence, on every house rooftop 'taken over' for security purposes, in every innocent 'razing' [of fruit groves]. People whose entire lives have been 'taken over' by the army, leaving them stripped of every right, without citizenship, delivered into our hands. But the worst is the roadblock. There you don't do anything evil, you just send everybody back the way they came. They can't leave their village. They can't move from their homes. With a wave of the hand, thousands of persons are held in confinement, denied work, starved, isolated, deprived of any chance of a normal life.

These evils aren't perpetrated by evil individuals (that kind have their own form of evil – curses, beatings, unwarranted shooting, the glee of 'treating' the Arabs, 'We'll show 'em at long last !') No, they are the evils perpetrated by honest leftists: the transparent evils, self-evident under occupation; impossible to erase. Impossible to evade, if you go there.

That is precisely the justification of the *intifada*: to make the occupation less transparent, not allowing it to be forgotten or vanish, to remove momentarily the forgetfulness that Israelis (Israeli Jews, that is) decline into the moment the shooting dies down. The settlers don't need to sublimate – they never forget the occupation; they enforce it in person. The ones who do need to are the lefties. They just don't like the occupation, so they simply forget it.

I run into this time and again, in all these discussions going around and around, and it amazes me: the occupation is transparent. It's a self-evident state of affairs, all the discussions are swallowed up within it. It is only out of total indifference to the context that one can talk about this 'sudden war' that the Palestinians forced upon us. 'Our task is to defend the settlers and protect ourselves.' Entire cities, dozens of villages, homes, hundreds of thousands of individuals – abruptly evaporate when we're on reserve duty. There is no sign of the people who have lived three and a half decades under occupation, without rights, their lives not worth tuppence. So there: transparency pays off. It's as though we were on Mars. As though there has never been an occupation that hasn't evoked resistance, and as though such resistance doesn't ultimately triumph.

## Second round

*'What would happen if everybody refused? You're like those who don't take antibiotics, and rely on others who do.'*

There are moments when reality prevails over sophism. Moral action is tested within its actual context, not in hypothesis. At this time (June 2001) there are a hundred refuseniks. Far too marginal a ratio. If there were three hundred or five hundred – long before the phenomenon becomes a 'real threat' – someone up there might realise he doesn't have enough soldiers to follow him blindly into a megalomaniac war to perpetuate the accused (and doomed) occupation. If there had been more refuseniks in the Lebanon war, it might have ended ten years earlier. If there had been more refuseniks in the first *intifada*, maybe the occupation would have ended long ago.

## Third round

*'But this is no joke, we're at war.'*

No point in repeating that a war is conducted by two armies, that war assumes some kind of symmetry, that war can be won on the field of battle. This isn't war, and therefore there is no 'military' issue to be decided; this is an uprising, in part armed, against an occupation. And after the manner of such uprisings, it will probably get fiercer. Therefore any child knows that there's no hope of an Israeli victory.

Occupation, not war. And how did you think it would end? Out of our goodwill, our Jewish morality? Prior to 1988, did anyone so much as imagine giving up the chance of bargain hunting in the lively markets of Gaza and Tulkarem? Did anyone so much as see the Palestinians a yard before his nose?

If this is war, what kind of war is it? What are its aims? Must moral judgement fall silent when the word 'war' is heard? When is one supposed to oppose it? Was the word 'war' supposed to have provided the justification in Lebanon for every reservist to bomb Beirut, or make thousands of villagers flee? So when does moral judgement come into effect – at your leisure? When it's peace and quiet out there?

# Yesh Gvul's *Survival Kit for Refuseniks*

The *Survival Kit for Refuseniks*, published early in 2002, is one of Yesh Gvul's most popular publications. Leaving aside ideological or political topics, it focusses exclusively on the nuts and bolts of refusal, aiming to de-mystify the process and reduce the terrors of defiance and prison, and thereby encourage those soldiers still in two minds to take the plunge into refusal.

The 16-page booklet advises reservists to give their unit advance notice of their intention to refuse service in the occupied territories; likewise, to report on the appointed day and at the appointed place, to avoid being tried as AWOL. The booklet reports that most refuseniks hitherto have not been disciplined. Those facing disciplinary action are advised to opt for trial by the immediate commander, whose juridical authority is limited to a short sentence. '*Precisely those officers close to your political viewpoint are liable to impose harsher punishment.*'

While in prison, the refusenik forfeits the reservists' allowance he should get from National Insurance, but he can apply for support from the Yesh Gvul family aid fund. The movement also offers to help the refusenik in his links with his family, and convincing family members riled by his act of refusal.

The booklet expands on military prison, pointing out that '*contrary to prevalent notions, jailed refuseniks do not suffer harassment by gaolers or other prisoners ... All our members who did time report that they were treated with respect.*' The booklet describes prison conditions and the daily round: 4–5 parades, and the choice offered between sorting military equipment, or not working. '*You can make use of your time for reading, preparing university assignments, etc. You are free to bring books, newspapers and writing materials without restriction.*'

Prison food comprises army rations, and prisoners get a daily allotment of 10 Noblesse cigarettes. Good conduct reduces one day in ten of your sentence (if you got 28 days, good conduct will set you free after 26).

The booklet sets out the routine for visits, lists numbers of public phones in the prison, and offers various tips on conduct there. '*Entry into prison may come as a shock to you. The warders put on a 'ritual' (yelling etc.) during the first couple of days, to flaunt their powers. But that usually passes after a few hours. You may be a little dazed for the first day or two, but the other prisoners will take you in and fill you in with basic know-how (when is there hot water, where is the best place to work etc).'*

Yesh Gvul advises the refusenik to make contact with the movement and have his name published in the media, to publicise his action. But if he declines to have his name made public, he will be treated discreetly and anonymously. To those undecided whether or not to refuse, the booklet recommends setting fears at rest by talking to a refusenik who recently did time in a military prison.

# Is Marwan Barghouti your uncle?
## Itai Ryb

*In April 2002, Itai Ryb, a physics student at Jerusalem's Hebrew University and a lieutenant in the reserves, served a one-month sentence for refusal to take part in the occupation. Since his imprisonment, Ryb has become a Yesh Gvul activist, working on the prisoners' committee.*

In the course of ten minutes with the deputy brigade commander, I managed to explain in an agitated murmur why I refuse to take part in the Israeli occupation (2 minutes); to hear his learned opinion about obedience and morality (5 minutes); and note the views of the brigade quartermaster about a solution to the consequent transportation problem ('Tell Avi to take him to prison in the Peugeot'). On the way to jail, I was asked why I was refusing, whether Palestinian politician Marwan Barghouti was my uncle, how much had the Nokia phone cost me, and so on and so forth. They were all in a hurry to get to Bethlehem, and get me to Military Prison No. 6. It was April 1 – April Fools' Day.

I refused to take part in sweeping the Palestinian problem away with excessive force, and in response, I got swept away myself. It wasn't so much that they wanted to punish me, it seemed they were more interested in rendering my protest banal, like the 'judicial' process I had undergone, like the 'prison' I was going to. Naively, I thought that the act of refusal was adequate and self-explanatory, but they took it as switching from the occupation game to the refusal game, so just as the 'judicial process' wasn't really a process and the prison isn't really a prison, my refusal isn't really

Itai Ryb, refusenik, outside Military Prison No. 6 in Atlit, where he spent a month.

refusal and the occupation isn't really occupation. That keeps everyone virtuous in their use of weapons, and ready for a loud argument in the family room when the war comes to an end.

It's easy to have a sensitive conscience when you're in jail; it's harder to keep your conscience free of pomposity and self-righteousness, a practical conscience commensurate with who I am, aware of how easy it would have been to patrol the streets of Bethlehem. Sadly, my conscience remains the same as it always was, but my daily round in prison already follows a different routine.

Today, two months after my release from prison, I see nothing of the change I hoped to bring about by means of my refusal. Dread over the unchanging political status quo was one of the most important grounds for my decision to refuse. I'm haunted by the feeling that I've heard and seen the selfsame headlines time and time again: as a child during the Lebanon war, as a boy during the first *intifada*, as a soldier in the Israeli occupation force in southern Lebanon, and as I am today. My refusal is, above all, a refusal to come to terms with a reality-without-solution.

The significance of the act of refusal and its impact have been written about by persons older and wiser than me, relating to over a thousand refuseniks and over twenty years of the refusal movement. In my view, the refusal of an individual under the given circumstances is one small, persistent step on the way to change, just as it's the sum of all the acts of collaboration and unquestioning conformity that have taken us this far down the slippery slope of thirty-five years of occupation, to the chasm where we find ourselves now. I have no wish to detail my objections to the oppression of the Palestinians, and my efforts for peace, or what happened to me last April in prison. I was no trailblazer, but I did prove that my path is the path of peace, and that is the path I shall follow. As I entered the prison gates, I was convinced that refusal is the only step I can take to reconcile my deeds with my conscience, with the overall rights granted to every human being, and the quest for a solution as a basic human behaviour pattern. On my release from jail, I was equally convinced that as long as the occupation and the callousness last, I shall persist in my refusal.

# Why am I mad at the IDF?

## Ron Gerlitz

*Rob Gerlitz served in the navy, achieving the rank of captain. He is employed with a hi-tech firm and active with both Yesh Gvul and Courage to Refuse, and is currently working in California.*

April 1996, Operation 'Grapes of Wrath' was at its height in Southern Lebanon. I was in command of a navy gunboat. The vessel went off for a routine daily tour far to the north. The boring and unglamorous 'security patrols' now gave way to operational tours opposite the Lebanese coast. The sea was ours, our blockade of Lebanon was in force, our assignments were exciting and we felt great.

And did I mention 'sense of mission'?

All this was ahead of the truly attractive assignment we had been given – to bombard the Lebanese coastal road, which was packed with vehicles. Most of them were fleeing northwards. Our task was to deter any headed south, though we should endeavour not to fire directly at passing vehicles (does this sound humane? Wait for the rest).

You don't have to be a ballistics expert to know that if you spend days on end firing alongside vehicles, ultimately you'll hit one of them. And indeed, one day we hit a car. Apparently, its occupants were killed. We took this indifferently (it's always convenient to adopt the plural in such situations).

Do you understand why I'm mad at the IDF?

Because the IDF sent me to shell a road used by innocent civilians whose only sin was that they were driving south to extricate relatives, since Israel was threatening to bombard southern Lebanon. Because the IDF sent me to take part in a 'war of choice'.

What did I do? I carried out my assignments; I was even enthusiastic about them. The only thing I can say in my defence is that when we officers had a briefing with the navy commander, I complained about the type of munitions we used! The answer I got was annoying and rather contemptuous, towards me and those at whom the shells had been fired.

I left the briefing for another night of bombardments, enthusiastic as ever. Adrenalin is an intoxicating drug, you should know.

What is it I can't forgive myself for?

Not for obeying orders. The way I was then, 23 years old, a product of the Israeli school system, an officer, a captive of the myth of the 'Israel Defense (?) Force' – all that made it very hard to say 'No'.

I've forgiven myself for carrying out my orders. But I haven't forgiven myself for having no doubts, no soul searching, not even for a single moment. Is it a moral act to shell innocent civilians? Is it permissible?

Is there a black flag of illegality over such an act ? Or is the flag dark grey?

Was I the latest in a long line of soldiers (in the IDF and other armies) who consent to take part in wars of choice and perpetrate inadmissible acts?

*If I had searched my soul*, it would have been O.K.

*If I had only had second thoughts about the order*, that would have been O.K.

*If I had thought about the dubious moral aspect of my assignment*, that would have been O.K.

*Even if I had ultimately decided to carry out the order.*

To my shame, I didn't even entertain the faintest shadow of doubt in my thoughts. That is something for which I cannot forgive myself.

What did I learn from that episode?

A very important lesson.

I learned that in one of the most important aspects of my grasp of life, I am inclined to confuse cause and effect. At one time, I believed that my acts were determined by my value system (or simply, my thoughts). Those nights in the spring of 1996 taught me, in retrospect, that the opposite is often the case. What I do is what frequently determines what I think.

I've noticed that when you're preoccupied from morning to night, bombarding a coast along which people are travelling, you end up convinced that it's the correct thing to do, morally justifiable. I found this an astounding and frightening discovery (and took it along with me to further years of reserve duty).

What is the practical conclusion ?

I am writing these lines dressed in IDF uniform. Yes, I'm on reserve duty, but I've learned that my moral standards must lay down the limits of my obedience. I've also learned not to take part in wars of choice. I've learned that there are things one mustn't do, even if they rest upon 'security

The second of a series of Yesh Gvul's 'survival kits' for distribution to soldiers, designed to resemble a military ID card and to fit into the shirt pocket of a uniform.

grounds' (genuine or false) – for it seems that every atrocity committed here is justified by some 'security grounds'. I have notified my superiors that I will take no part in naval actions against the Palestinian population in the Gaza Strip. The occupation is in total negation to my values and complying with it contradicts my comprehension of democracy. If I am sent, I will not go.

## What about Zionism?

On the one hand, we believe that the existence of the Israeli state is justified and we desire its wellbeing (what people round here call 'Zionism'). On the other hand, principally due to matters I have described, we tend to believe that whatever we do in the army is for the benefit of the state (whether we believe in the assignment, or just think we should carry it out to comply with the rules of national decision-making).

It's here we've run into a contradiction.

The occupation regime is a security disaster, its perpetuation a grave blow at national security. Due to the occupation, fresh graves are dug every day.

Accordingly, our service for the occupation regime effectively operates against the national interest, and is therefore an anti-Zionist act.

Zionism is a movement for the creation of a safe democratic homeland for the Jewish people. A state moving on a non-democratic course does not implement Zionism. The state's treatment (in practice) of the Palestinian 'Other' as inferior in worth – is undemocratic.

Millions at our mercy – that is undemocratic.

Sieges, closures, administrative detention and torture – all that is undemocratic.

Hundreds of roadblocks denying the Palestinians basic human rights such as freedom of movement, the right to medical attention, as well as the right to dignity – they are really undemocratic.

All of the above are immoral, undemocratic and therefore operate against Zionism. I have begun to feel lately that the state has begun to slide down into a military and moral chasm, with unforeseeable consequences. I feel that it is our duty to halt that decline.

What is Zionism right now?

It's refusal to take part in the occupation.

# The Gaza bombing was a war crime!

*In July 2002, Israeli airforce combat planes bombed a residential quarter of Gaza, with the professed aim of killing a Palestinian militant. The one-ton bomb dropped struck its target, but also killed numerous innocent civilians, including children and a baby. The shocking event provoked a measure of unease and criticism in the Israeli public, which official spokesmen tried to deflect into a technical discussion of bomb size, distances, blast and fallout. Yesh Gvul brought the focus back to the moral and humanitarian level with the following advertisement in Ha'aretz:*

---

There's no need for 'technical' details (calculation of distances, size of bomb or 'timing'), for the blood cries out;

There's no need for a commission of inquiry, for it is clear beyond any doubt who gave the order, and who carried it out.

THE GAZA BOMBING WAS A WAR CRIME AND THOSE RESPONSIBLE MUST STAND TRIAL:

Prime minister **Ariel Sharon**, who took the decision;
Defence minister **Benyamin Ben Eliezer**, who confirmed it;
Chief of staff **Moshe Yaalon**, who recommended it;
The **airforce squadron commander**, who issued the order;
And the **pilot** who dropped the bomb.

If the Israeli judicial system is incapable of undertaking the task, those responsible should be indicted by an international court.

Saturday 27 July 2002, outside Military Prison No. 4, Yesh Gvul will hold

A VIGIL IN SOLIDARITY WITH THE JAILED REFUSENIKS

Come along and support the IDF soldiers who refuse to take part in the campaign of repression in the occupied territories!

---

# Closing Statements

## My reply to the General

### Yigal Bronner

*Yigal Bronner teaches South Asian Literature at Tel Aviv University. He is active in Ta'ayush – the Jewish-Arab partnership which extends humanitarian and political support to the Palestinian population in the occupied territories. Bronner has taken a leading part in the Ta'ayush campaign on behalf of a community of cave-dwelling shepherds in the South Hebron area.*

> General, your tank is a powerful vehicle
> It smashes down a forest, it crushes a hundred persons
> But it has one defect
> It needs a driver.
> BERTOLT BRECHT, 1938

Dear General,
You wrote to me recently that 'in view of the extended state of war in which we find ourselves ... and in view of the resultant operational requirements', I am summoned to 'operational duties in the Horon sectors'. I am writing to let you know that I have no intention of responding to that summons.

During the eighties, Ariel Sharon erected dozens of colonies for settlers in the very heart of the occupied territories, a *démarche* whose ultimate aim was the utter repression and dispossession of the Palestinian people. Today, those colonies control close on half the area, stifling the expansion of Palestinian towns and villages and preventing the movement of their

115

inhabitants. In this new century, Sharon – now prime minister – is preparing the final stages of that project. He has dictated the operational orders to his scribe, the minister of defence, and from there they were transmitted down the chain of command.

The chief of staff declared that the Palestinians are a cankerous threat and gave instructions to subject them to chemotherapy. The head of Central Command gave instructions to impose a curfew of unlimited duration. The brigade commander stationed tanks on the hills and between the houses, and forbade Palestinian ambulances to evacuate their wounded. The battalion commander announced that the rules of engagement ('open fire orders') would henceforth read: '*The order is – open fire!*' The tank commander observed a number of persons residing in a suspicious manner in their homes, and ordered the gunner to blast off a round.

I'm the gunner. I'm the final small cog in the wheel of this sophisticated war machine. I am the last and least link in the chain of command. I am just supposed to obey orders. To reduce myself to stimulus-and-response. To hear the command 'Fire !' and squeeze the trigger. To burn it into the awareness of every Palestinian. To complete the grand *démarche*. And do it all with the natural simplicity of a robot who senses nothing beyond the shaking of the tank as the shell is ejected from the gun barrel and flies to its target.

But as Brecht wrote further:

> General, man is very useful
> He can fly, and he can kill.
> But he has one defect.
> He can think.

And so, *mon général*, whoever you are, battalion commander, chief of staff, minister, prime minister – one or all of the above – I am capable of thought. Maybe I can't do much beyond that. I have to confess that as a soldier, I'm not particularly gifted or courageous. I'm not a good marksman. My technical abilities are minimal. I'm no great sportsman either, and I can't even get my uniform to fit me too well. But thinking is something I'm up to.

I can see where you're leading me. I can understand that we shall kill and crush, wound and die, and it will never end. I know that 'the extended state of war in which we find ourselves' will extend on and on. I can deduce that the 'resultant operational requirements' require us to hunt down and starve an entire nation. Something about those 'requirements' has gone badly wrong.

Therefore I have to turn down your summons to duty. I won't come along to squeeze the trigger on your behalf.

Of course, I have no illusions. To you I am a buzzing gnat that you will swat and try to crush before striding on. You'll find yourself another gunner, more obedient and gifted than me. There's no shortage. Your tank will rumble on. One single gnat can't halt a tank, certainly not a column of tanks, certainly not the entire march of folly. But the gnat can buzz, irritate, infuriate, occasionally even sting. Ultimately, more and more gunners, drivers and commanders, who will see more and more aimless killing, will also start thinking and buzzing. There are already many hundreds of us. Ultimately our buzzing will ascend into a deafening outcry that will echo in your ears and the ears of your children, and on the pages of history for many generations.

So general, before you swipe me away, maybe you too should do a little thinking.


# Israel today is a prison

## Matan Kaminar

*Matan Kaminar, jailed December 2002 for his refusal to enlist, comes from a long line of political activists, among them his father Noam, who was a refusenik during the Lebanon war and one of the founders of Yesh Gvul. This is Matan's 'going to prison' statement:*

Freedom is, among other things:
Riding the bus and looking at the sea, or reading a book, totally at ease. Walking the land and knowing each part of it, without knowing fear. Meeting new people of all sorts and becoming friends. Finding a job I like and which pays a living wage. Studying what I want to without having to pay a fortune. Rejoicing in Israel's human variety without worrying about so-called demographic or economic threats. Walking down the street, or waiting for the light to change, or standing in line at the supermarket, without being drowned in commercials. Hearing the news without hearing about innocent people getting killed.

A place without freedom is a prison.

Israel today is a prison.

The worst kind of prison is the invisible kind. We cannot see our prison, not because it's bewitched but because we are blind. Our capacity to sense suffering has been blinded. First we were blinded to the suffering of people who look very different from us: they live up in the mountains, they wear moustaches and veils, and they apparently hate us because we are more beautiful and intelligent than they are. Then we were blinded to the suffering of people who look more like us, and even talk our language, albeit in strange accents. But I guess they're not as able as us, and that's why they have no jobs and their children have no food. Lastly, we have been blinded to our own suffering. We've been convinced that we don't really suffer – what doesn't kill you makes you stronger, and hey, we're not dead yet. We've been blinded to think that our agony is pleasure, and that depression is fun.

The most suffocating kind of prison is made of glass.

Today I'll be going to another kind of prison, a kind made of cement and tent canvas, of barbed wire fences and the uniforms of prison guards. It's called Military Prison No. 4. I'm glad to be going because, finally, my prison will be visible. I'll do my time in this visible prison for a few months for refusing to enlist in Israel's academy for prison guards: the IDF, Israel's 'Defense Forces' which have been imprisoning an entire people for thirty-five years.

In Military Prison No. 4, I may develop a miraculous sense of sight. From staring at the fabric of my tent I might gain the ability to see fabrics of deceit. Looking at cement walls may teach me to recognize the walls separating human beings. Seeing barbed wire may bring me understanding of the wiring by which people are controlled.

Hope and experience both show that sight is an infectious trait. My goal is an epidemic of seeing people who will tear down the walls of separation with their sense of sight. They will use their vision to rip away the canvasses of lies, and cut the wires of exploitation with their eyes. Military Prison No. 4 already holds a few people who are trying to see, sitting and looking and waiting for me to join. In the schools and on the buses, in the refugee camps and the factories, on the streets and at the roadblocks and in the offices, thousands of seeing people are already infecting their neighbors with the seeing virus.

Soon a critical mass of seeing people will have collected. All of a sudden, everyone will be able to see the prison. Even the guards will realise that they, too, are prisoners.

And the prison will be gone.

# ● List of Addresses

**Yesh Gvul** can be found on
*www.yesh-gvul.org*

The *Shministim* (high school students) can be contacted via
PO Box 70094
Haifa 31700
Israel
or
*shministim@hotmail.com*

The **Courage to Refuse** declaration by army reservists can be found on
*www.seruv.org.il*

# Zed titles on Israel/Palestine

- Esther Benbassa and
Jean-Christophe Attias
**The Jews and Their Future:
A Conversation on Judaism
and Jewish Identities**
1 84277 390 9
1 84277 391 7

- Marwan Bishara
**Palestine/Israel: Peace or
Apartheid Occupation, Terrorism
and the Future** UPDATED EDITION
1 84277 272 4
1 84277 273 2

- Uri Davis
**Apartheid Israel:
Possibilities for
the Struggle Within**
1 84277 338 0
1 84277 339 9

- Nicholas Guyatt
**The Absence of Peace:
Understanding the Israeli-
Palestinian Conflict**
1 85649 579 5
1 85649 580 9

- Hussein Abu Hussein and
Fiona McKay
**Access Denied:
Palestinian Land Rights in Israel**
1 84277 122 1
1 84277 123 X

- Peretz Kidron
(COMPILER AND EDITOR)
**Refusenik!
Israel's Soldiers of Conscience**
1 84277 450 6
1 84277 451 4

- Ephraim Nimni (EDITOR)
**The Challenge of Post-Zionism:
Alternatives to Israeli
Fundamentalist Politics**
1 85649 893 X
1 85649 894 8

- Rosemary Sayigh
**Too Many Enemies:
The Palestinian Experience
in Lebanon**
1 85649 055 6
1 85649 056 4

For full details of this list and Zed's other subject and general
catalogues, please write to: The Marketing Department, Zed Books,
7 Cynthia Street, London N1 9JF, UK; or email
sales@zedbooks.demon.co.uk

Visit our website at: http://www.zedbooks.co.uk